P9-BZY-438

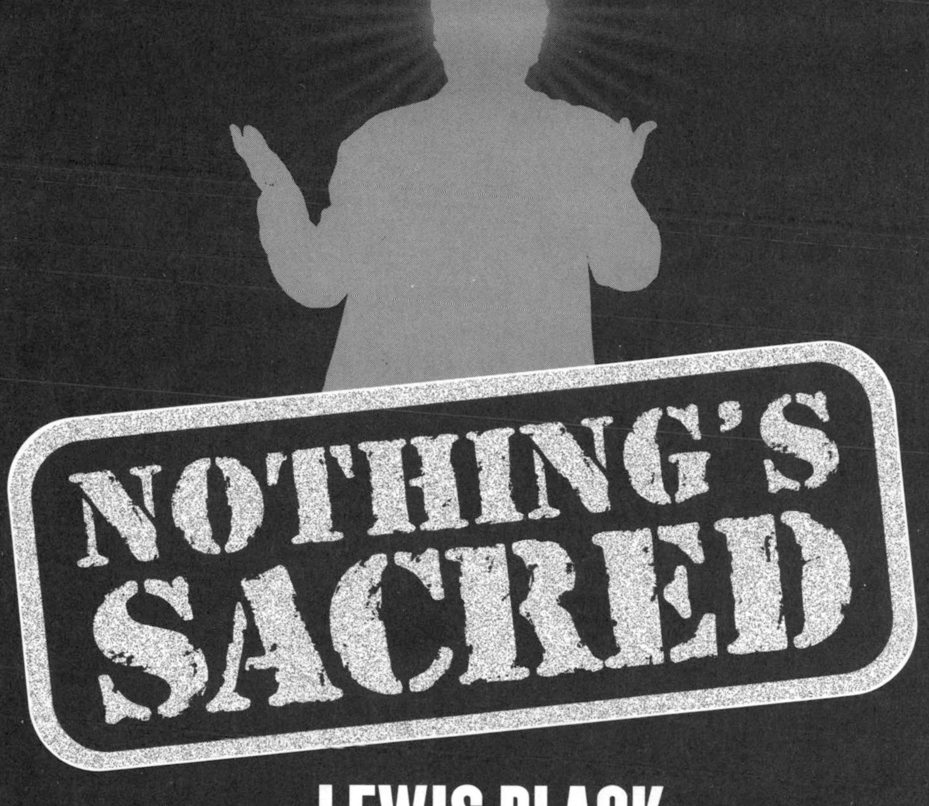

NOTHING'S SACRED

By **LEWIS BLACK**

Edited by Hank Gallo

SSE SIMON SPOTLIGHT ENTERTAINMENT
Simon & Schuster, New York

New York London Toronto Sydney

With grateful acknowledgment to Paul Krassner for granting his permission to reprint an excerpt from "The Parts Left Out of the Kennedy Book" copyright © 1967 Paul Krassner.

SSE

SIMON SPOTLIGHT ENTERTAINMENT
An imprint of Simon & Schuster
1230 Avenue of the Americas, New York, New York 10020

Manufactured in the United States of America
10 9 8 7 6 5 4 3 2
Library of Congress Cataloging-in-Publication Data
Black, Lewis, 1948-
Nothing's sacred / by Lewis Black.
p. cm.
ISBN 0-689-87647-5
1. American wit and humor. I. Title.
PN6165.B63 2005
814'.6--dc22
2004027808

This book is dedicated to all of my friends who helped me get to where I am today—you know who you are . . . and when I find you I am going to kill you.

INTRODUCTION:

WHY I HATE AUTHORITY

What am I doing writing a book? I can't sit still for that long.

For reasons that now escape me, I wanted to be a foreign service officer. Who knows, maybe I thought it was glamorous, or maybe the idea of travel just appealed to me. (I doubt I was really interested in shaping American foreign policy; that sounded too much like work.) I soon discovered how many requirements there were to qualify for a job in foreign service, and that's when I decided that I wanted to be a writer, because there were no requirements. All you had to say was, "I am a writer," and you became one. You didn't even have to write anything. You could just sit in a coffee shop with a notebook and stare into space, with a slightly bemused look on your face, judging the weight of the world with a jaundiced eye. As you can see, you can be completely full of shit and still be a writer. Okay, maybe that's the one requirement.

I also thought it was going to be a great way to meet girls, but it wasn't—probably because as I was staring into space, I no doubt looked mildly retarded. You see, I wanted to write plays, which in retrospect is a lot harder than learning Mandarin, I think. How I ended up in this delusional state shall be saved for another time.

Eventually I began to fill the pages in front of me with words. It was exciting. It was romantic. And yet I felt like I was losing my mind, listening to voices in my head while trying to overcome years of lethargy by sitting and stewing in my own juices for hours. My brain was constantly humming with a little voice that would cry out, "Are you insane? Who would want to read this drivel of yours, let alone perform it? There are real jobs even you can do and contribute to society. You are insane, aren't you? You just want to end up in an asylum somewhere, where they will take care of you." And in the twenty or so years that I wrote plays, I made less than I would have if I had chosen to be a migrant worker.

And so after years of playwriting, I became a successful comic. Go figure. So imagine my surprise when Steve, my agent, called and asked me if I wanted to write a book. Without hesitation I said, "Of course I want to write a book." But my brain was shouting, "You're insane."

Doesn't everyone feel they can write a book? Doesn't everyone feel that with just a few tens of thousands of well-chosen words they could put the Earth right back onto its proper axis? (Maybe that's not the case nowadays; maybe everyone just wants to be on a reality TV show and have people write about them.)

With so many more places to drink coffee nowadays, I leaped at the opportunity to share my insights with the world. Ask someone to write a book and that person's ego knows no bounds.

After years of working as a comic, I know how to talk funny. But can I write funny? So that the words leap off the page in such a way that the reader is filled with glee?

You don't know till you try, and there are legions of critics ready to tell you that you aren't funny in the least.

So what was I going to write about . . . ? Certainly not politics, as the shelves are filled with wonderfully funny works that have successfully covered that subject, by writers from Art Buchwald to P. J. O'Rourke to Michael Moore.

I am no David Sedaris or Dave Barry or Mark Twain. Jesus, Mark Twain—not only was he funny, but he's dead and he's still funny.

I picked up a cup of coffee and stared off into space. It's not so romantic when you actually have to have thoughts and write them down, especially now that I apparently had a severe case of ADD. My head just couldn't wrap itself around a topic, because I got bored immediately with any topic that came to mind. In my desperation to come up with an appropriate subject, I even considered writing about interior decorating, which I know nothing about.

Then one day, while sitting on a plane, headed to God knows where, I had a revelation. I am constantly in the air sitting next to guys who are about my age, and they talk to me as if I am twenty years younger than they are. And they seem twenty years older than I am. They always seem to have sticks up their asses. Where was my stick, I wondered? Where did the stick come from? Was there something inherent in being an adult that I had missed? Why did so many of my generation seem to have gone on to become joyless and officious snots? How could Dick Cheney and George W. Bush be around my age and yet it was as if we were living in parallel universes? Was there something wrong with me that when I heard the words "get on board" I would rather drown? It's not a question of politics. It's deeper than that. It has to do with our points of view, the way we look at the world. Where did mine come from?

That's what this book is about. Maybe I am emotionally stunted, but by the time I was in my early twenties I had developed the way I look at life, and it hasn't changed much since then.

This is the road I traveled, as I remember it—which may not always be accurate, since as I have gotten older my memory has become a blender.

And so we begin.

SUBURBIA

"Everybody knows this is nowhere."
—Neil Young

I was born in Washington, D.C., on August 30, 1948. For those of you who believe in such things, my birth date makes me a Virgo, the sign of the anal-retentive. The sign kind of sucks, really, and I don't know if it has helped or hindered me, but I am sure the stars do more than twinkle.

I was raised in Silver Spring, Maryland. Of course, there is no spring there, and I can assure you no one was mining for silver. Its only claim to fame is that it is the largest unincorporated city in America. In other words, we were too lazy to govern ourselves. Our town motto was "I'd like to vote, but I don't feel like driving."

Silver Spring is a suburb of Washington, D.C., and all suburbs are identical. The houses may vary in size and design, but the game is the same. Everyone has the feeling that they are living in a special space, when in fact there is nothing unique about it. Being brought up in suburbia is, therefore, like being born and raised nowhere. It is an oxygenated void. As a result, it prepares you for either depression or space travel. Have you ever heard of the great suburban writer? Well, I promise, you never will. I can just imagine how chapter three would begin. . . .

So many leaves, so little time. I will buy a leaf blower.

Growing up in suburbia, everyone was middle class. Everyone had a lawn and a car. Everyone was white. Except for the maids, who would arrive once a week to clean up after all of us. It's what I imagine South Africa was like during apartheid. There was a wide variety of white people, though—Italians, Irish, Poles, Russians, Jews, Catholics, WASPs. It may have been sterile, but we all seemed to get along.

It was the fifties and America was booming. It was a time when father actually knew best and there was a sitcom to prove it. Elvis Presley was changing the genetic structure of America's children. There were TV dinners specially made, I guess, for watching TV.

The USSR, however, presented a bit of a problem to the idyllic suburban American lifestyle. It was our sworn enemy and it was going to bury us. They were evil—really evil, spectacularly evil. So evil, in fact, that if you had ever been a Communist, you were tainted for life, or so said Senator Joe McCarthy. Communists apparently walked among us, like aliens, ready to convert us to their heathen ways at any opportunity. The Commies were no better than child molesters. I didn't experience that level of paranoia again until I smoked pot.

I never quite grasped this concept; my family came from Russia, and if they were any indication of the Soviet mentality, I didn't think we had much to worry about. My grandfather had come to the United States in 1916 and didn't realize he was here until 1967.

Worst of all, the Soviets had the atomic bomb, and they were going to use it if they thought it was necessary. The good news was that we also had the A-bomb, and if the Ruskies got out of line, we would blow them all to kingdom come.

At school we kept getting mixed messages about the atom. It was used to create the weapon that blew the shit out of Hiroshima and Nagasaki, but according to a Disney cartoon, *Our Friend the Atom,* the atom was the best thing since sliced bread. It would, we were instructed, eventually answer any problem with which civilization was presented, including the need for mass annihilation.

It was all very confusing to my seven-year-old mind. It was a cartoon. It was really sweet. And it was Walt Disney telling me this, for God's sake. Uncle Walt! The same Walt Disney who had given me Mickey, Donald, Davy Crockett, and my first introduction to entertainment-related marketing.

It turns out that Disney produced this nonsense with the help of the US Navy and General Dynamics, the folks who built the nuclear submarine USS *Nautilus,* which carried nuclear missiles. Imagine Halliburton and the Department of Defense using *Beauty and the Beast* to sell the war in Iraq to elementary school students. In case you weren't sure, we'd be the Beauty.

I didn't know what to think. Especially given the fact that we were being shown instructional films on how to protect ourselves in case of nuclear attack. They would show us image after image of A-bomb tests and even the real deal at Hiroshima, just in case our childlike minds couldn't grasp the devastation caused by these weapons.

Other films demonstrated how to protect ourselves in case our neighborhood just happened to take a hit. And living outside Washington, D.C., that was a really good possibility—even a second grader could tell you that. These films would show a bomb blowing the ever-loving snot out of everything in sight, a fireball of epic proportions that let off a monstrous blast of heat. It turns out, though, according to the powers that be, that all you had to do to protect yourself if you couldn't find proper underground shelter in time was "duck and cover."

That's right, just duck down and cover your head, and you could survive the blast. Yeah, sure, right. Even I knew after watching these films that you might survive, but your face would no doubt melt and your nose would probably end up on your foot.

We would even have air-raid drills once a month in my school. It was, perhaps, the kindest way for the administration to remind us we could all die at any minute. So, all of my little friends and I would hide under our desks to protect ourselves. And all I could think while I was under the desk was, *What are these adults who are in charge of me thinking? I am not a goddamn idiot!*

We are talking about a fireball from hell, and these morons had me hiding under wood—under kindling, for God's sake! I might as well have been a rump roast in an oven. Looking back, I now know it was at this point in time that I began to regard authority with a jaded eye. I don't know what these people were thinking. Just because they were completely stupid, I was supposed to be stupid too?

If that weren't dumb enough, bomb shelters became all the rage. People were building underground cubicles in their backyards where they could hide in case of nuclear war. There, they could stow food and water and wait for the all-clear signal to sound. It looked good on paper, but the idea of spending weeks in a tiny room with my parents and brother just didn't seem worth the effort.

Not to mention the fact that there was also the possibility that those without shelters would try to break into yours. Luckily my parents had a basement, which saved us the embarrassment of building a shelter. Even though we were told to keep food supplies down there, we didn't. My parents seemed to have the same idea I did: If the bomb were dropped, then the hell with everything.

The folks who told us we could protect ourselves from a nuclear attack by hiding under our desks are the same jackasses who just told us that we could protect ourselves from a chemical attack with duct tape. Yeah, if you had enough to wrap yourself in, you could suffocate before the chemicals got to you.

So underneath the calm and peaceful serenity of the suburbs was a sense of uneasiness that pervaded our lives. It was the kind of feeling you get when you're at an elderly woman's apartment, where there is a scent of roses in the air that just barely masks the smell of death. Even though she may be giving you sweets, you still feel queasy.

Also really popular at the time were toy guns. Along with my friends Ed and Stan and a bunch of other kids, I played cowboys and Indians. This was during the Davy Crockett phase of the fifties, when every child who wore a coonskin cap was instantly transformed into an idiot wearing roadkill. We played cowboys and Indians not as some sort of racist activity—it just made the cap make sense. Besides, there are no Indians in the suburbs.

We also played war, which meant we divided up into two squads and spent the afternoon killing each other. It was splendid—and it was just as much fun killing your pals as it was when they killed you.

It should be noted at this time that not one of us ever had an interest in real guns or ever bought one. Then when it came to raising kids, my generation didn't allow them to play with guns. That's when things took an abrupt turn for the worse. I certainly wouldn't say there is a connection, and I don't know what changed in our culture, but it is strange that only a few kids play out these war fantasies in their backyards and yet there seems to be more violence among them.

On those Saturdays when we weren't pretending to protect the world from the Russian onslaught, we attended double features, usually horror films, much to our delight. But they were never as scary as we had hoped. We were like junkies for fear, always in search of a good scare. But the aliens were never alien enough and the monsters were never monstrous enough to satisfy our cravings. I don't know what drove us to return week after week, only to go home disappointed.

And God knows what we would have done if we were really scared. Our lives were nice, really nice. Maybe that forced us to crave a little of what wasn't nice, to shake us to our roots and make us pee our pants. Nothing, I guess, was scarier than the specter of a mushroom cloud.

HALLOWEEN

It's scary for all the wrong reasons.

I'm not big on Halloween. I never have been. As a kid my parents would send me out to collect for UNICEF, which just screws up the whole holiday. You're wearing a costume and people are giving you pennies and you're going, "Well, give me some candy, you fuck." And the grown-ups tell you, "Absolutely not. You've got your pennies. Now go build a village, you little shit." It still brings a tear to my eye.

If you are an adult and you wear a costume on Halloween, *stop it.* I don't know when adults decided to play dress up—talk about disturbing. And let's get it straight: It is not your holiday. It's for kids. You see, kids would like to put on a costume every day if they could. That's why we have Halloween, so we can say to them, "Listen, you little prick, today is the day."

It makes no sense that we celebrate Halloween in urban areas. It's a harvest holiday, and in New York City, where I now reside, we don't harvest shit. Halloween in New York is redundant. "Let me put a costume on over my costume and a mask on over my mask."

And what's with the pumpkin? What's so festive about a gourd, and why would anyone carve a pumpkin more than once? That's why they have plastic pumpkins. I can remember the only time I carved a pumpkin. As soon as I cut into it, an odor permeated the room, which made me ask, "What died in there?" The pumpkin emits one of the worst smells in the universe, and if it came with a mouth like a jack-o'-lantern, it would say, "Don't open me."

I don't believe pumpkin pie is even made from pumpkin. I mean, how can something that smells that shitty make a pie so sweet? There's not enough sugar in the universe.

It's one thing to be driving through a rural area late one moonlit Halloween night and pass a farmhouse with a big smiling jack-o'-lantern in the window. When any presidential candidate speaks, he is speaking to that person who lives in a farmhouse with a smiling pumpkin in the window. That's where they think we are all living, huddled around the fireplace, listening to ghost stories. And that's why we have trouble understanding what they are saying to us.

It's another thing to live in New York City and walk down the street on Halloween, where there isn't a pumpkin in sight except for one tiny smiling pumpkin on the thirty-fourth floor of an apartment building. How creepy is that!

But nothing proves just how stupid we are as a people more than candy corn. Which, by the way, is not candy at all. You can actually melt it down and run a car. I think it's tar-based. Candy corn is the only candy in the history of the country that has never been advertised. It just appears.

I'll never forget the first time my mother gave me candy corn. "Here, you're going to love this, Lewis, because it's corn that tastes like candy." I put it in my mouth and thought, *This tastes like shit! My mother's fucking with me.* So I ate another, and it tasted like shit too.

Still, every year Halloween returns and I find myself in a room confronted with a bowl of candy corn. And even though I have seen it every Halloween of my life, I still stare at it as if I've never seen it before, like an Alzheimer's patient. "Wow, candy corn—corn that tastes like candy. God, I can't wait." I take a bite and—"Son of a bitch!" Then I do what every American does. I grab another and just eat the yellow part, stupidly thinking that it's the corn part and that those other colors are what ruin the taste. Then I take two more pieces, turn them so the pointy ends are facing down, push them onto my teeth, and pretend I am Dracula.

Here's a little-known fact: All the candy corn that was ever made was manufactured in 1904. That's because we don't eat enough of it and we throw most of it away. So the candy corn company sends out their representatives in early November to gather up all the discarded candy corn from the Dumpsters and bring it back to their factory, where they simply wash it off and bag it up again. A year later the same candy corn is on every coffee table in America.

Many of you reading this have children, and the rest of you may eventually have children. Halloween will come and you will give them the corn that tastes like candy even though you know that it tastes like shit. And so it goes . . . from generation to generation to generation, we pass on a legacy of shit.

And then you wonder why we can't elect good leaders.

THE PLEDGE OF ALLEGIANCE

. . . with liberty and Starbucks for all.

It is utterly amazing that people have the time and the energy to argue about the wording in the Pledge of Allegiance, specifically the words "under God." That phrase seems to get them all worked up in a lather, especially the atheists, who love to keep bringing this to the table for discussion.

Yet I've known a lot of atheists in my life, and none of them has ever seemed interested in this ongoing debate. Where does an atheist get the energy for this kind of activity, anyway? They don't even have the energy to have faith, for God's sake.

The "under God" was added to the pledge during the fifties as a kind of vaccination against the godlessness of Communism. Well, guess what? We don't have to worry about Communism anymore.

And the fact of the matter is, as far as I'm concerned, it doesn't matter whether kids say it or don't say it. You see, they're just kids, they don't know what they are saying. The concepts in the pledge are way beyond the grasp of children. It sounds important, but it's senseless to a child, especially at eight o'clock in the morning. And no child, ever, has said the words "under God" and experienced the rapture. To put it simply, the pledge of allegiance is like a cup of coffee for elementary school students: By the time they finish saying it, they are awake enough to realize they are in school.

When I was in school, we used to say the "Our Father" prayer as well. It was like a much-needed second cup of joe. A lot of people are still very upset that kids don't have to recite it anymore. Well, I said that prayer every morning at school until I graduated, and it had absolutely no effect on my life whatsoever. None whatsoever. Amen.

JUDAISM

We created the concept of guilt.

If religion is the opiate of the people, how come so many Jews seem more neurotic than sedated? My childhood was a time of anxiousness, and religion never provided me with any solace. My religion was Judaism, even though very few of my relatives actually practiced it. Most of them didn't attend temple on a regular basis. They were good for the major holidays—the big four, as I call them: Rosh Hashanah, Yom Kippur, Hanukkah, and Passover. By Jewish standards, that would not be called being a practicing Jew, but it was still enough reason for the Russians to kick their asses on a regular basis.

My maternal grandfather's family even moved to Israel—or Palestine, as it was called back then. Apparently my great-grandfather decided he had a year to live and wanted to die in Palestine. Nobody really seems to remember how he came to that conclusion. He packed the whole family up, and at the start of the twentieth century they left Russia. A year passed, and my great-grandfather was sill alive. That's when my great-grandmother said, "Enough is enough," and moved back to Russia with the family, leaving her husband alone in Palestine.

Meanwhile my grandfather had decided he hated Russia and felt that Palestine was a hellhole, so he headed off to America instead. After the move to the States, he

LEWIS NILES BLACK

Temple Sinai

invites you to worship with us on

the occasion of our

Eleventh Confirmation Service

Shavuot, the sixth of Sivan, 5724

Sunday, the seventeenth of May, 1964

ten o'clock in the morning

3100 Military Road, Northwest

Washington, District of Columbia

was never too keen on Judaism, or any religion, for that matter. Ironically, his name was Israel.

In spite of my grandfather's ambivalence, my parents decided to raise my brother and me in the Jewish religion—probably to give us an idea of our cultural heritage. Also, the inescapable Jewish guilt no doubt just made them feel obligated to do so. Either way, it worked. There are things about the Jewish religion that I carry with me to this day.

Chief among them is Yom Kippur, or the Day of Atonement, as it's so happily called. It had a profound effect on my innocent young mind. The service opens with the organ playing "Kol Nidre," one of the spookiest pieces of music ever written. You hear it and are literally surprised that bats and shit aren't flying around. I think Alfred Hitchcock based all of his film scores on it. As the service proceeds, you learn that Yom Kippur is the day that one atones for all of the sins that were committed over the past year. "This," the rabbi intones, "is the day that God puts your name in the Book of Life or the Book of Death."

How sweet is that? The Book of Death! Are you kidding me? That's a hell of a concept for an eight-year-old to deal with. Until then my own death wasn't something I had even considered. So what flashed across my mind as I recounted my numerous sins (which were conveniently printed in my prayer book) was an aged God with hands trembling as they hovered over the Book of Death. In one of those arthritic hands I imagined a pen. And as he got closer to the book I saw his hand shake ever so slightly and watched as a drop of ink fell to the parchment. I further imagined that God stared at the drop for a moment and, almost as an afterthought, in the most beautiful cursive penmanship proceeded to write the name, "Lewis Black."

In short, the whole idea of a Book of Death rattled the bars of the little cage that was my existence. I became obsessed with it, and I set out to prevent God from making any mistakes when it came to me. I was going to make sure that I never had another bad thought or did a bad deed, figuring that was all it would take to make God leave me alone. Considering I was just eight, there really wasn't much I could do to stop God from doling out the ultimate punishment. But since I was, in fact, merely eight years old, I didn't know that.

So I came up with a plan. Whenever I had a bad thought I had to immediately say, "I am sorry, God." I did this for a while, but then I figured it might not be enough. That's when I decided to add, "Please forgive me." This, I thought, was the only way to make sure that God would have to participate.

In truth, I hadn't really had very many bad thoughts until I heard about the Book of Death. When I knew of its existence, however, it seemed I couldn't stop having them. I wished ill health on my teachers. I wished that my classmates would flunk their tests. I wished that my parents would like me more than they liked my brother. I wished for a lot of bad things. I don't really think I wanted the bad things to happen; I think I just wanted God to know how sorry I could be and maybe give me some extra credit.

This lunacy on my part grew in leaps and bounds. It was no longer enough to say, "I am sorry, God. Please forgive me," just once. No, in just a short period it became five times, and then ten, and then it grew to multiples of ten. I couldn't be sure how much "sorry" God really wanted from me and I wanted to give him as much as possible. At first this was all done in silence. But soon I felt compelled to whisper it, as if God needed to hear me to know that I really meant it.

I then continued to embellish my tapestry of prayer. I added an inhale after "God" and an exhale after "me." Soon this became the major activity of my life. I wasn't paying much attention in school anymore because I was too busy fending off an angry God to worry about spelling, math, or my notebooks. I might as well have been spending all day at the temple, because there I sat in the midst of my class, davening away like an Orthodox Jew.

The classmates who sat near me must have thought I was nuts. And I was. My grades began to plummet and my parents began to worry. I was taken to a counselor. I have no idea what kind of counselor, but he was definitely some sort of adult authority figure. I don't remember him; I just remember stopping the behavior. I was probably more afraid of my parents than I was of God.

And therein lies the problem with Yom Kippur. It doesn't take into account the highly vulnerable trigger mechanism of a child with obsessive-compulsive disorder.

But Yom Kippur wasn't the end of my religious training. I attended Sunday school until I was confirmed, which meant I went until I was fifteen. My dad had made a deal with my brother and me. He would attend lectures on Judaism every Sunday and we would go to Sunday school. Once we were confirmed, the bargain went, we could decide if we wanted to continue practicing the faith of our fathers, as would he, depending on how he felt at the time. In retrospect, as long as he was negotiating, I should have cut a better deal. What I should have said was, "Let's call the whole thing off after my bar mitzvah." Unfortunately I wasn't thinking ahead.

In that time, I realized the really nice thing about Judaism—and Catholicism, for that matter—is that it removes you from society and, for all intents and purposes, puts you in the role of the outsider for a brief time each week. It therefore helps you empathize with those who are different from you. Not bad, considering I was being raised in a country where as much as people want to be the same, they are truly different. Understanding that you are different also helps you feel a little bit special, and that's a good thing. Unless, of course, you are living in one of those neighborhoods where if you are a little bit different, they like to kick your ass for the fun of it.

What makes the Jewish Sunday school experience different from all other religious training is the haunting memory of the Holocaust. We Jews don't ever want to forget—or let the world forget—what happened in Hitler's Germany. It's an admirable mission that is excellent in theory but can be borderline insane when it comes to practice. You see, the adult Jewish community wanted us kids to know all about the Holocaust; so on a very regular basis from around the time I was ten, I was exposed to one documentary after another. And each seemed to feature some of the most horrific footage known to mankind.

The names of the camps were pounded into my head, like a train schedule to hell: Treblinka, Bergen-Belsen, Auschwitz, Dachau. I don't think it was really very healthy for me to be viewing that footage in the innocence of my youth. No, not good at all. By the time I was twelve, I felt like I had seen every Jew killed about eight times over. Combine this with a reading list on the subject, and I am amazed I can walk without braces on my legs or a breathing apparatus trailing behind me on wheels.

I did have a great rabbi, though, named Balfour Brickner. He is the only one who seemed capable of bringing me across the great divide to an understanding of how the Bible affected my life. It was the driving force behind his social activism, and that, coupled with his charm and charisma, made the guy a triple threat. I even thought seriously of becoming a rabbi, even though I felt utterly damaged by my religion. I probably just wanted to have a congregation to yell at, in retaliation to what I felt I had suffered in my own temple.

But when Balfour left, we got a new rabbi. He didn't bring much to the table, but as with most guys of the cloth, his heart was in the right place. He wasn't cool, though, and I desperately wanted to be cool, or at least lukewarm. By the time I was bar mitzvahed I was done with Judaism, even though I made some real nice coin that day. I even thought my parents and I should make it our life's work—move from village to village, where Jews were dwelling, have another bar mitzvah, pocket the change, and roll on out of there.

One of the things I think religion should provide is hope. Judaism provides an awful lot—and the moral standard it gives us to live by is, was, and will always be astonishing—however, hope is not big on the list. Not when you've got a Yahweh who is always on the verge of blowing a gasket. He's a lot like Ralph Kramden—if Ralph Kramden had minions and even knew what minions were. You just could never do enough for the guy. He's like a Jewish mother run amok. For example, he told his first true believer, Abraham, "It's not enough to sacrifice a goat or sheep. Bring me your son." Are you kidding me? You can philosophize all you want, but that's nuts. Moses spent forty years leading the Jews through the desert to find the Promised Land, and when he finally did, God said to him, "You're not getting in. You can kiss my ass."

And look at the story of Job. After that one you have to wonder why you'd ever go to temple to pray again. Since Job had absolute faith in him, God singled him out and decided to test his faith. Sure, Job was an upright man, but God, who back then had time for these things, decided to see just how faithful he was by taking away everything the guy had. Then, when Job had nothing left, God gave him boils and still Job kept his faith.

Call me silly, but I think you like to get out of a system what you put into it. You've got to question a God like that, don't you? I sure did—enough to stop listening for an answer. Given his personality type, I thought it was for the best.

And we Jews have no heaven. We have a vague messianic age—key root of the word, messy. The messiah will come at some point to usher in the age; we just don't know exactly when. Well, after you put that message out, wouldn't you expect a Jesus of some sort to arrive on the scene? Ultimately we got a Mel Gibson, but we're still waiting on a Jesus figure.

I mean, the messianic age is a nice concept, sure. But death seems so . . . final. I think the notion of heaven or ideas about reincarnation give one a little something to hang on to. Hope, if you will, which is especially welcome if you are stuck on a Greyhound bus for thirty-six hours. My hope came from music, but that didn't happen until later.

CATHOLICS

These are the people who codified guilt.

The Catholics have it right. I love what they do. That whole "the pope's infallible" thing is tremendous. Let's face facts: If you took somebody with no religious leanings whatsoever and locked that person in a psych ward with nobody around and no stimuli, the Catholic religion is exactly what he'd come up with.

"Listen to this. There's this old guy in a dress, see? He wears all these great costumes and whatever he says, about anything from birth control to what to watch on television, that's it, 'cause pope knows best. He can't lift his head up, but, fuck, he's a genius."

But my favorite part of that religion is the act of confession. I've always been jealous of that. Catholics can fuck up all they want then go in a week later and tell the priest, "Oh, well, Father, I fucked up." And he says, "Hey, buddy, it happens. Here—eight Hail Marys and a side of fries, and you're home free."

There is something so perfect about that. I just can't understand how the priest figures out what kind of penance to dole out. Is there a list somewhere? If you commit adultery, it's so many of this, and if you use the name of the Lord in vain, it's so many of that. I can only speculate that when the priests are in the seminary their teachers say, "Here—memorize this list. You're going to need it."

But what happens if some special circumstance comes along? For argument's sake, what if a guy fucks a monkey? I guess they have to call the pope. . . .

"Hello, Your Holiness, this is Father O'Reilly from New York. . . . Fine thanks, yourself? . . . Well, Your Eminence, I've got a sticky one here. You see, one of my congregants fucked a monkey earlier this week and he wanted to confess. The problem is, monkey fucking is not on the penance chart, so what do I do? . . . No, he didn't mention if the monkey was Catholic. Is that important?"

THE PROTESTANTS

And these are the folks who transformed guilt into "tension."

The contribution of Protestantism to religion is the concept of the potluck supper, and without the Protestants, there would be no Christian Right. So some questions should be asked, but I haven't got the time to bother asking them.

GAY MARRIAGE

"Don't wear green and yellow on Thursday, its Queer's day."
—An old high school proverb

If there is one group of Americans that takes a beating from religion, it's the gay population. They finally get out of the closet and who's there to welcome them? The Bible thumpers, nuts of the highest order. Many believe that this is one of the major reasons Bush the Junior won the election. Well, that and the fact that Kerry couldn't figure out how to beat a man who was already beating himself. Eleven states voted to ban gay marriage. I guess it's the step you have to take first, before you clothe the naked and feed the hungry.

The issue of gay marriage is kind of complicated for some people. I don't know why, but it is. One reason might be that there are large numbers of people in this country who have never met a gay person. Or, if they have, they just don't know it.

You may be one of those people. You may never know that a gay guy is pumping your gas or running the local bank or living right next door to you. Hell, you may even be married to a gay guy and don't have a clue. Don't believe me? Well, next time you're in New Jersey, have a little chat with Mrs. McGreevey.

In short, there are still plenty of places in this country where, in bar after bar on a Saturday night, somebody will eventually stand up and say, "If a faggot came in here I'd kick his ass!" And this is what makes many gays so cagey. Most of them are too smart to hear that and respond, "Here I am, you savage!"

And I'm not just talking about rednecks here. Even Rick Santorum from Pennsylvania, a well-educated man and one of the highest-ranking Republicans in the Senate, doesn't have a clue. Instead of just shutting his mouth because he didn't know anything, he actually said that homosexuality was a threat to the American family. Of course, he didn't explain why, he just said it as if it were written in stone.

Did I miss something? I read a lot, but never once have I heard about groups of gays hopping in vans and driving from suburb to suburb, threatening American families. If only somebody could convince Santorum this isn't the case. But in his demented mind, he has apparently convinced himself that these same gays are driving into culs-de-sac from coast to coast, jumping out of the vans, running into houses just as families are settling in for their evening prayers, and fucking each other in the ass in front of the kids.

Of course, if it were happening that way, I could understand how families could fall apart and within six months show up on *The Jerry Springer Show.* Who could blame them? But, like I said, I read a lot, and when I'm not reading, I watch *The Jerry Springer Show.* A lot. So far, I'm happy to report, there is no concrete evidence to support Santorum's claim. Nothing.

So for that portion of Americans like Santorum, who for some idiotic reason have a problem with gay people, gay marriage sends them around the fucking bend. It just flips them out, which raises the questions: What's the problem? And who cares?

We've already allowed gay people to adopt kids, so the ball game is basically over. If you wanted to raise any shit on this issue, that's when you should have raised it. If you didn't, just move along. And after 9/11, you can't tell me that gay marriage is the biggest worry we have. "Oh no, the gays are getting married! Let's go to code orange." By my calculations, on the list of things we have to fret about, gay marriage is on page twelve after "Are we eating too much garlic as a people?"

And I think it takes a lot of balls for heterosexuals to make a fuss over this issue, considering 50 percent of us can't even stay married. It's not like we have a lock on this institution. For all we know, if gay marriages were figured in to the equation, the divorce statistics may even go down. That's actually one of my secret dreams because it would be a hell of a kick in the ass to the religious right.

But back to reality. Just what did our illustrious forty-third President, one George Walker Bush, contribute to this argument? A proposed constitutional amendment stating that a legal marriage has to be between a man and a woman. As with many of his ideas, this was a very, very bad one. After all, a thousand years from now, we don't want the next civilization to unearth our culture and find this sort of legislation. I mean, after they take five months surmising what Ronald McDonald was up to ("Burgers and children? What was the connection?"), they'd take a look at the Constitution and they'd say, "Look at this, marriage is between a man and a woman. These people were so fucked up they actually had to write it down so they wouldn't forget."

So why do Bush and his Christian buddies believe marriage is between a man and a woman? Because it says so in the Bible—the Old Testament, to be exact. Of course, they've forgotten we have a thing in this country called "the separation of church and state" or, as I like to call it in layman's terms, "the tough shit law."

But they also seem to have forgotten that the New Testament is the Christian Bible and the Old Testament is the Jewish bible. Please allow me to speak on behalf of my people: "Keep your fucking Christian Right noses out of our reading material!"

Now, to be fair, there's a good reason why the Old Testament states that man must marry woman. It's because, at that time, the Jewish people weren't civilized, and the Bible was, in large part, written for that very reason—to civilize people. So the leaders were forced to come up with a God who was such a prick he could keep those peckerheads in line. And I don't want to get any mail about this, but we were, as a breed, only ten hairs away from being baboons back then. So they came up with this really scary God and a list of rules, and they told everybody that God was there to enforce those rules.

They needed to do this because as the Jews were wandering around willy-nilly in the desert, one of them no doubt led a camel up to a rabbi and said, "I met her at an oasis and it's been wonderful. She looked at me in a way that I've always wanted to be looked at. We're in love and, well, Rabbi, we want to be married."

And the rabbi said, "Perhaps you didn't notice, but she's a fucking camel." Then he went back to the other rabbis and informed them, "Son of a bitch, we have to come up with another rule! Today a guy came back with a camel and yesterday one of them showed up with a snapping turtle. God knows what's going to happen tomorrow. We've got to get these people on track." Hence, the man-woman marriage rule in the Bible.

But just because it's in a religious doctrine doesn't mean we, as a nonsecular country, need follow it. After all, Americans must never forget there is a much higher law that governs us—the tough shit law. It's a really good one.

WASHINGTON, D.C.

The seat of idiocy

No matter what they say, D.C.—like it or not—is a Southern city. It's got an easy, slow feel to it, and there is always a touch of drawl in the air. Maybe things have changed a bit with the influx of a million lobbyists, but back when I was growing up in the area it was most definitely the South.

As intimidating and sterile as some of the government structures may be, there is a serene beauty to the city, provided by the wide expanse between the Lincoln Memorial and the Capitol. Even for someone as cynical as I am, the memorials are oddly inspiring. They serve as a reminder of just how far our leaders have strayed from the roots of democracy.

I wish members of the federal government would take five minutes each day to wander down to the Mall and take a look at Lincoln and Jefferson. But maybe those guys were pricks too. I can only imagine what a memorial to Bush or Reagan would be like a hundred years from now. For all we know, a whole new generation will be in awe of those idiots.

The problem I always found living so close to D.C. as a kid was that the government was always in your face. It could make you crazy. The morons start spouting nonsense, and because you're close by you just want to drive downtown, find them, and start screaming at them. If I had lived there as an adult, I probably would have lived over a grate near the Capitol building so I could yell at them every day.

It doesn't help that there is a new president every four to eight years, because the town goes through a whole sea of change with each newly elected commander in chief. Whatever tastes the president brings with him are reflected in a slew of new restaurants and retail stores. The town never holds its own against the president. It's his show. It's his style. It's his town. And Washington has always suffered for it.

I have always felt that they should have built a monorail in D.C. rather than a subway. Not that the subway isn't a splendid piece of work. It's just that Washington might have been better served if it could see itself anew.

One of my funniest experiences in D.C. was the bicentennial celebration in 1976. I went down to the Mall with some of the old gang, looking forward to the music and especially the fireworks. What a catastrophe. The sound system sucked, the laser light show was a bust, and the fireworks were a fiasco. The fireworks were the last straw. We could hear them, but they never made it over the trees. We went from Americans attending a celebration to an angry mob taking to the streets. They were lucky we didn't burn down the city that night.

One of my most extraordinary experiences in D.C. was the afternoon I saw Martin Luther King Jr. give his "I Have a Dream" speech. I was a hundred yards from him. I may not have fully comprehended the moment, but I knew I was in the presence of greatness.

But my finest moment was probably when my friends and I took off our clothes and strolled buck naked around the Jefferson Memorial. It was a beautiful summer's eve and if people noticed, they didn't seem to care.

In my youth it always amazed me how bad the slums were in D.C. They were the worst in America and they sat right behind the Capitol. Our leadership was confronted daily with this serious problem and never did anything about it. They just walked on by and eventually paid a little lip service from the podium. Nowadays those slums are gone because of urban renewal. But other slums still exist in D.C. They're just better hidden.

MY MOTHER

"Next time, I'll raise dogs. They are more loyal and more excited to see you."
—Jeannette Black

Jeannette is her name, and she was a teacher. Actually, she wanted to be a biologist. She got her master's, but it turns out that today, her master's is just a few credits shy of being a Ph.D. She isn't happy about that. Apparently back in the late thirties and forties, when it came to education they weren't kidding around; you actually had to show real knowledge over an extended period of time and number of courses. You can't do that in today's high-speed world; people don't have the patience. "Just give me the degree and let's get on with it."

She began her teaching career in an all-black school in the District of Columbia. You see, this was in the early fifties, the heyday of an absolutely shameful segregationist policy called "separate but equal." I like to call it "separate but equal my *ass*." Imagine that, in our nation's capital, right in the midst of all those lawmakers. The mind reels in the face of such racist nonsense and the stupidity of the leadership that fostered it.

With her biology degree, my mother was, of course, teaching high school math. There was a curriculum in place that was supposed to be followed religiously. But my mother, being a gifted and intelligent woman who was ahead of her time, slightly modified the curriculum. She wanted to be sure her kids knew why they were learning math and give them a practical application for a science, which those kids didn't seem to have. So she would take them to stores, give them an amount of imaginary money, and ask them to figure out what they could buy with it. This also allowed her the chance to teach them to be intelligent consumers.

The powers that be found out what my mother was doing and reprimanded her for going outside the curriculum. She argued that the curriculum was a sealed vacuum unto itself, one that turned the kids off the subject entirely. Many of these students were not going to end up in college and desperately needed a practical application for math in their environment. The administration told her do it their way, and she responded by taking the highway. As you can see, by railing against authority I am hardly breaking new ground in my family.

It wasn't until my brother and I were older that she began to teach again. She became a substitute teacher for the county where we lived, which meant she spent a lot of time teaching in my high school. Talk about a potentially inflammatory situation. The last place on earth you want your mother is at your high school, and certainly not as a substitute teacher. Substitute teachers may as well walk into the classroom with targets on their backs. Being the son of one certainly puts a kid in harm's way. Kids have been beaten up with much less provocation, such as wearing green and yellow on Thursday or knowing the answer to a question that no one else did.

But I was lucky. Make that very lucky. My mother was really good in the classroom—any classroom, with any kind of kid. A lot of my fellow students didn't realize I was related to her, because they thought if she was my mom, I should have been a whole lot smarter. My mother never had any problems controlling her students because nobody, and I mean nobody—not even the snottiest peckerhead or the biggest thug—could stand up to my mother's sarcasm. It was withering and unrelenting. It came from a place deep within her DNA. Thousands of years of Jewish irritability and humor went into the genetic masterpiece that comprised my mother's snide barbs.

She could deliver a line like it was a heat-seeking missile, crushing whatever the problem might be, in an instant, amid gales of laughter. She left no prisoners. She was legendary. Students actually hoped they would get her as a substitute. After a class of hers, word would spread in the hallway of some off-the-cuff remark she had made to put down whatever wiseass was dumb enough to try to disrupt her class.

The bottom line is, my mother is funny. I mean, seriously funny. Heart-stoppingly, belly-achingly funny. Her humor comes from my grandfather, who was never happy but always funny. His three most famous quotes were: "It's a great life. You're born in Russia and they bury you in New Jersey." At the height of the Vietnam War, he said, "If I knew it was going to be like this here, I would have stayed in Russia." And when the tax men came to his business in 1967 because he never paid taxes, they said, "You have to pay taxes every year," and he responded, "Really? I didn't know."

My mother is cynical like H. L. Mencken, only while in the classroom she didn't have the luxury of crafting a line at a typewriter. She had to whip it up in real time, in front of the toughest audience on earth—high school kids.

Once, a student in what was the toughest classroom at the time asked why he had to learn whatever subject she happened to be teaching that day. Without missing a beat, she said, "Because when you are pumping my gas at the Sears Station, where you have been for ten years because you didn't get your diploma, I don't want to have to waste any breath saying 'I told you so.'"

When my friends would gather at my house, my mother eventually would get around to her favorite speech. The one where she would tell us that we were never going to be any better off than our parents. That family is a wonderful thing, but ultimately it's what makes any real change impossible. We would, she would go on, all be compromised into oblivion. It was the kind of conversation that went great with snacks.

My mother didn't like to cook when I was growing up, and it showed. The food was scary at times. Vegetables would be hot on the outside and frozen in the middle. Beef was cooked to a point of appalling grayness, and gravy didn't exist. The whole idea of the happy homemaker of the fifties had made nary a dent in my mother. She found the notion preposterous. To her, being happy as a homemaker meant you needed a round of electroshock.

She once cooked a meal, however, that was so unforgettable that years later I asked her why she never cooked it again. She said it was because we liked it. There is one thing that can be said for her cooking: It prepared me for industrial cooking, that's for sure.

But my mother dished up a sense of humor that has served me in good stead, and that beats a good home-cooked meal anytime.

TELEVISION

Global village, my ass!

As far back as I can remember, we always ate dinner with the television turned to the news with Walter Cronkite. My mother would heap a torrent of abuse on the TV whenever some piece of nonsense irritated her. (This got much worse as we moved into the Vietnam War.) And since Walter spoke more than my dad, at times I felt maybe he was my father.

During my childhood we went from black-and-white television to color television. Things became a bit more confusing after that. Black and white kept everything simple. You could see the good and you could see the evil. With color you could never be too sure.

And with the invention of the remote, ADD was no longer just for kids. I think the condition actually began with the invention of the clicker and got worse with the birth of cable. Things went completely over the top when every news channel decided that listening to a human being wasn't enough, so they added the scroll on the bottom and as much other crap as they could possibly fill the screen with. It's like an information salad bar, and like most salad bars, it's not healthy.

MY FATHER

"Boomer Sooner, Boomer Sooner, Boomer Sooner, OK U!"
—University of Oklahoma's Fight Song

My father was and still is a quiet man. My mother shoots from the hip, but my dad is very thoughtful. He can usually be found with an impish smile on his face, as if he's perpetually watching a dirty movie.

Sam was a mechanical engineer. His dad died in the huge influenza epidemic in 1918, when my father was one year old. He was raised by my grandmother in New York City, where she had landed at the age of sixteen after leaving Russia, and while my father was an only child, he was brought up in a houseful of cousins, aunts, and uncles.

When it came time to go to college, my father found the cheapest school of engineering, as far away from New York as he could get. Culture shock be damned, he went to the University of Oklahoma. I cannot fathom leaving New York City and going to rural Oklahoma, but as an only child, I guess culture shock was easier to deal with than my grandmother. She was a lovely woman, sweet to a fault, but she carried that delightfully subtle guilt of the Jewish mother like a claw hammer. So my father probably went west, like many others, to find himself and get some breathing space.

My father loved the theater. My mother liked it too, but he really adored it. It quickly became my love as well.

He took me to my first play in New York City when I was about twelve—*The Golden Fleece,* starring Tom Poston, a cast member of *The Steve Allen Show.* We'd go to eight or ten plays a year together, and I became more and more fascinated by the theater. From the best to the worst, it didn't matter to me.

We saw *The Wayward Stork* in the early sixties, a play about a mix-up in a sperm bank and the high jinks that ensued. I'll never forget it. It was one of the worst plays I have ever seen. No one was laughing except for one guy, dead center front row; he was convulsed by every awful joke. I asked, "Who is that guy?" My dad replied, as if on cue, "He's the playwright."

During World War II my father wasn't drafted, because he worked for the War Department as a designer of weapons—sea mines, to be precise. They look like beach balls with stubs and are used to keep ships from entering the harbor. After the war and his subsequent marriage to my mother, my father tried desperately to get work designing in the private sector, but he had two strikes against him. First, he was Jewish, and anti-Semitism still prevailed among America's manufacturers. Second, most of the country's manufacturing had switched from consumer products to weapons, and my father wanted out of that line of business. Unable to find the kind of work he was looking for, my dad remained a government employee and continued to work on sea mines.

As our country slowly began to drift further into the Vietnam War under Johnson, my mom began to work for the Women Strike for Peace. My dad was not as quick to jump on the antiwar bandwagon as my mother. He picked up the Geneva Accord and actually read it—something

I'm pretty sure Johnson never did. This document was supposed to be the basis for our going to war, and my father read the whole thing to see if there was some rationale for our being in Southeast Asia. I tried to read it but got through about three pages—it was like reading some sort of psychotic legal contract.

When my dad finished going over it, he said there was nothing in it to justify our going to war. A few years later we mined the North Vietnamese harbor at Haiphong. It deeply upset my father. He was always able to work on sea mines in good conscience, since it was a weapon whose purpose was supposed to be purely defensive. Now they had become offensive weapons in a war that had no real justification.

My dad was fifty-three at the time. I was in college and my brother would be there in a year. He decided to retire at the age of fifty-five, ten years before he had planned to. It was truly an extraordinary event for a man with a family to give up his income in order to be able to live with his conscience.

When your father drops out of the mainstream economy because of his principles and pursues a dream, it profoundly changes the way you look at the society in which you live. I didn't realize all the ramifications of his decision at the time, but it left a lasting impression on me and shaped the way I looked at work and what it meant. I was thrilled because my father was truly a role model for the sixties. He was hip. He was a dropout.

And so he retired and began to study the art of stained glass as an apprentice. He created works of his own and then began to study art at the local junior college. He took art courses there for more than twenty years. He became an artist and painted into his mid-eighties. When I asked him why he stopped, he said he had run out of ideas.

My father called his work hard-edged abstractionism. Don't ask. But if you know the work of Mondrian, who basically painted squares of color, you'll have an idea of what his work looked like. By far my father's finest work, as far as I am concerned, was a more realistic piece called "Show Biz." It's the only piece for which he ever wrote a title. When I asked my father what he really liked to do, he said, "Sit on a bench in Paris, France, and watch people walk by."

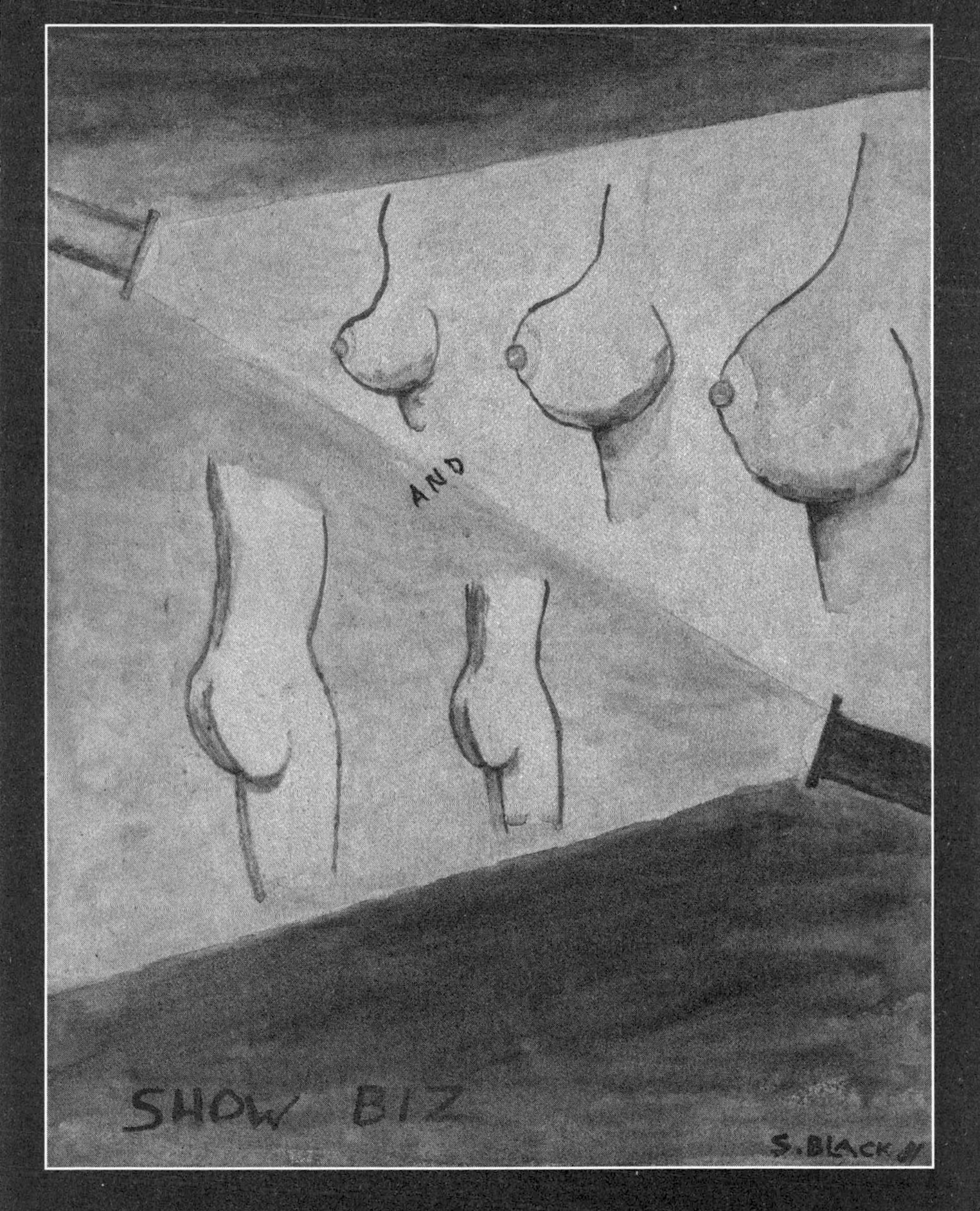
AND
SHOW BIZ
S. BLACK

MY BROTHER, RON

The good* do *die young and pricks* do *live forever.

If it weren't for my brother, Ron, you'd never have read a word of this book. I would never have been a comic. I would never have spent the amount of time I did working in the theater. He was a prince among men. He was an old soul, who knew the worth of this life. He was a noble soul, which means he appreciated the nobility of all around him. He was the essence of intelligence and humility, two traits that rarely appear simultaneously.

He was my best friend, and the fact that he isn't here to read this pains me more than anyone will ever know. This is his book. He didn't write it. He allowed me to live it. He supported me financially and emotionally. He was the best, and anyone who ever knew him knows that. His smile spoke more than any words could express. His love for me made this all possible. I am lucky we shared the same womb.

He was my younger brother, so as we grew up I was constantly beating up on him. Case in point: I was six, Ron was three, and we somehow had been given a gun with rubber darts. I had Ron stand against the wall, and I shot the darts around him. I then had him shoot at me. He hit me. So I beat him up. It was like that for a long time.

Ron became president of the student body in the eleventh grade, and my friends and I helped him with his campaign. He won again as a senior. He was a leader, something I could never achieve. One of his major accomplishments was a smoking lounge for students. He died, we think, of lung cancer, and that's the definition of ironic.

One night at our favorite New York hangout, the West Bank Cafe, we found ourselves arguing over the presidential candidacy of H. Ross Perot. My brother had decided to support this idiot and I was incensed as much by his choice as by the fact that our political fortunes had sunk so low. We had a huge screaming argument fueled by too much wine, and we hurled invectives back and forth about the state of the union. We were, as always, enjoying every minute of it—much more so than the rest of the restaurant, which we had brought to a complete an utter silence and of which we took no notice. I ended the argument by screaming at the top of my lungs, "Okay, you do that. You vote for H. Fucking Ross Perot. And you know what I'm going to do? I'M GOING TO TELL MOM!"

I was with my brother the night he died. We had a long chat, but in retrospect, I should have said so much more. I returned home, and just as I got in the door there was a call from his wife, Susan. He had taken a turn for the worse and it didn't look good, so I returned immediately. By the time I got there, he had ceased to exist. My sister-in-law said that the doctors thought that we should try mouth-to-mouth resuscitation. So I did, I tried to breathe life back into him, but it was useless. While I was doing so, it occurred to me, that if I brought him back he would no doubt be pissed and would start a long argument over how I could never leave well enough alone. The strangest thing is, I felt his presence in the room the whole time I was there, like he had not left. And he never really has.

We were intensely close and extremely different. Ron understood that differences between people were something to heal; I thought they were something to make fun of. He knew that life was something to be enjoyed, and I thought it was something to be understood. He was right. He was always right.

MY UNCLE JULIUS

The only one in the family with any rhythm, he was our Fred Astaire.

Julius was my mother's brother, a truly handsome man who became my role model. He wasn't like my parents. He wasn't married. He didn't seem to want to get married. He got a big kick out of life and truly relished it.

He was always dating a different woman. They were always full of life, and they were all stunning. I will never forget a picture he had in his Upper East Side apartment, which was the place to be in the early sixties. It was of him dancing with a beautiful woman. He spent his weekends in places with exotic names like Tanglewood. They don't use this word anymore, but the man was dapper.

Having served in World War II, he hated the Vietnam War. "These guys are so full of shit," he would say. At nineteen he had fought in the Battle of the Bulge, but he'd never talk about it. Julius was among the troops that had marched into and liberated Paris. That's something he would talk about. "Paris was good," he would say, "really good."

Julius always had a great car—a Jaguar or a Mercedes. We had a Ford Fairlane. There is no comparison. He was an optometrist and he was cool. How, you ask, can an optometrist be cool? I'm still not sure, but he pulled it off. And if an optometrist could be cool, so could I.

I was already halfway there. I was already wearing eyeglasses.

JUNIOR HIGH

If there is a hell, it is modeled after junior high.

Junior high was a huge transition for me. First, there were breasts. Of all shapes and sizes, as far as the eye could see, lovely, wondrous breasts. Elementary school had not prepared me for breasts. I was overwhelmed. And it didn't help that I had no cool. I was completely devoid of it. Nowadays being devoid of cool seems to actually make you cool. Back then it made you square.

For a time I was a square squared. My mother dressed me in irregular clothing and my pants were always way, way, way too baggy. When I asked why they were so big, my mother, as God as my witness, replied, "Because you have a big crotch." If this was the case, none of the girls in my class ever took note. Maybe because the top button of my shirt was always buttoned and I wore big tortoiseshell glasses. So I looked like a dump truck in heat.

Luckily I had a friend named Ray who set me straight. One day he pulled me aside and said, "You're a borderline asshole, you know that?"

"Just borderline?" I replied.

"You're salvageable."

"Where do I start salvaging? What should I do?"

"For starters, unbutton your top button."

I did, and I could breathe. Blood rushed to my head. I could feel my cool rising. "That's it?" I asked.

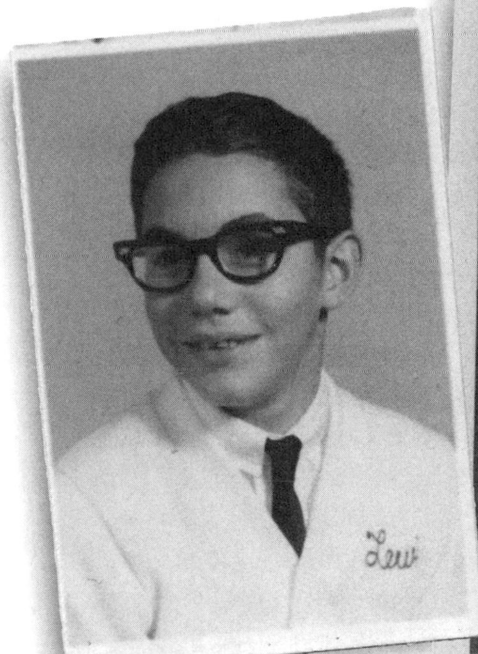

AAA

SCHOOL SAFETY PATROL

Award of Merit

This certifies that

Lewis Black

has served as a loyal and valuable member of the School Safety Patrol, helping to protect schoolmates from traffic dangers.

1961-1962

George R. Hammond

Manager, Traffic Safety Dept., District of Columbia Division, American Automobile Association

Springbrook School 3125

"There's more. Stop being so eager to please; you don't have to answer every question a teacher asks."

"I don't?"

"You are the king of the brownnosers. It's like you're constantly showing off, and nobody likes a show-off. You're smart. People know that. Stop worrying so much—you'll get good grades."

It took some effort, but I found my hand going up less frequently. This was not an earthshaking moment in my life, but it changed the way I saw things. I began to look less and less for the approval of authority figures. Between this and loosening my top button, I could breathe a little easier.

HIGH SCHOOL

The real world is just like high school, only there are more places to eat.

The assassination of President Kennedy was like a huge drug overdose, and by that I mean it changed the reality we were living in. Death is like a drug to the living in that it alters our perception of life. A public death of such magnitude is overwhelming to the senses and the mind.

Everyone seems to remember where they were when Kennedy was shot. I was in the tenth grade, but for the life of me, I can't remember which class. What I do remember is that the speaker on the wall at the front of the classroom, from whence all official pronouncements came, began to crackle with barely audible sentence fragments from a radio broadcast. You could just make out the words "Dallas" and "president." It was all very eerie, as everything that came out of that box was always crystal clear. It was like a transmission from an alien craft.

I may not remember my teacher, but I do remember her tears. "The president's been shot." I didn't believe it. It was unthinkable. There are no breakdowns of this magnitude in the suburban way of life. "President Kennedy is dead." I shed no tears because this could not possibly be true. My life was set up for safety, tranquility, and peace, and our lives were meant to be as orderly as our lawns. Now that was all over. Nothing, and I do mean nothing, would ever be the same. There was a tear in the universe.

My friends and I were merely numb for the next few days. We had no words to describe our feelings, because we didn't know what our feelings were. We played a lot of football under gray skies. We watched the interminable footage in black and white. I watched Lee Harvey Oswald get shot again and again and again. They couldn't kill him enough.

For the first time in my life, everything was out of control. My television had gone mad. This had been my comfort zone. This is where father knew best and they left it to the Beaver. What was next, a shootout on *American Bandstand*? There no longer seemed to be any rhyme or reason to our lives. So we played football. It was a simple distraction, for none of us were equipped to deal with the images that were flickering across our television screens. The bottom had fallen out and we were lost between adulthood and childhood, on a makeshift football field, as the sky grew darker and darker.

And as my world seemingly began to crumble, my sense of humor began to blossom. The genetically bred cynic that I was began to acquire the joy of the properly placed sarcastic remark. Nothing develops one's sense of the funny more than the hard reality of trauma. It's how we deal with the overwhelming shock—it helps us hide from it and, in a weird way, it's how we heal. Humor is how we find comfort in the totally illogical, for it is the bridge back to the logical.

And after trauma, the funny gets a whole lot darker. My sense of humor is how I got through high school, so you could say that President Kennedy's death made me enjoy my time in high school. Because after going through that kind of madness, high school was a piece of cake.

All my high school friends had one thing in common: They were very funny people. A few of them had started a cartoon book, drawn from personal experiences and the world that we were living in. These cartoons were at times very filthy, but boy, were they fiercely funny. The book moved into a higher gear when a fellow student of ours, sadly, killed himself. He was to us merely a face in the crowd, as he was new to our school. Suicide was something that none of us could really fathom, and so there was cartoon after cartoon pondering what brought this young man to such a sad fate.

It seemed to my friends that our fellow student was really looking for that perfect orgasm when he died. The kind achieved while one is suffocating. This was a whole new concept to all of us, an alternative to our tawdry attempts, which were certainly not taught in our health class. No doubt any adult who saw these cartoons would be totally appalled and demand that we each seek psychiatric care.

As time passed, these cartoons evolved into more and more depraved images—the sicker they got, the funnier we found them. One in particular comes to mind, of Christ on the cross, minions as far as the eye could see. He was smiling and singing a tune, while sporting a huge boner and ejaculating on Romans and worshippers alike. It filled two full pages and made us scream with laughter. It was sick, for sure, and I'll concede that you probably had to be there.

This type of nonsense wouldn't be tolerated today, not after Columbine. We, this group of very intelligent and well-behaved high school students, would be seen as half-crazed insensitive monsters that are liable to do anything. After all, the casual onlooker would be convinced we obviously had no real value system. But they would be wrong, because we did have a system of values, and it was called finding the funny.

Speaking of Columbine, what amazes me about the incident is, where did these kids get the self-confidence to perform such an act of violent retribution? Where did these kids get off thinking that everyone else was wrong and then finding the nerve to act upon it? When I was a kid, the loner was the one who had the courage to kill just himself.

I think we truly need to train parents. Apparently they have completely lost any sense of what the role entails. These kids were in the garage constantly, a public family space, and no one checked in to see if they wanted lemonade or some sugar-laden snack. They had enough weaponry between them to make a run into Baghdad, and their parents were totally oblivious.

Shouldn't the parents be held responsible? Are we completely insane? Am I? For God's sake, aren't parents the responsible party here? If we are going after the bartender who serves too many drinks, can't we at least harass the idiot who doesn't watch over his own child? Jesus, when I was a kid, my parents weren't overbearing, but they certainly paid attention when I took out my chemistry set.

When I was in high school, I liked laughing a lot. I wanted to laugh. I began to collect and listen to albums of stand-up comics. There was Bob Newhart, Shelley Berman, George Carlin, and Jonathan Winters. I'd watch Ed Sullivan every week to see the comic he had on. I was obsessed with laughter, and if someone had said I'd end up a comic, I'd have laughed in his or her face.

But I think what attracted me to the comic mind was the ability to pick up on the absurd. Or, in the case of the brilliant Mr. Winters, to show just how absurd the absurd could be. I had begun to a sense a glitch in the matrix of my life, if you will, and comedians were the first to point me in the direction of just where that glitch might be.

My search led me to subscribe to a satiric magazine called *The Realist* by Paul Krassner. It affected and shaped my young impressionable mind in ways unimaginable. I cannot for the life of me remember how I stumbled upon the magazine, but it was more precious to me than all the breasts that *Playboy* could deliver.

It was a pathologically dark humor magazine, for which Mr. Krassner was the inspiration, publisher, and primary source. I'll never forget opening one issue and there, smack dab in the middle of the magazine, was a panorama of all the Disney characters. It was seemingly harmless but, on closer inspection, you realized every one of them was doing something utterly perverse. Dumbo is taking a dump on Donald Duck. Goofy is screwing Minnie Mouse. Grumpy is shoving it up Dopey's ass. He had taken the Vatican of children's lore and cut it down to size. Disney, I heard, wanted to sue him but eventually changed its corporate mind. This taught me never to trust anyone who doesn't have a sense of humor.

Still, I shrieked. I howled. I couldn't wait to share this newfound treasure with my friends because that's when I realized their cartoon books weren't insane. They were satire.

I promptly became hooked on the way Mr. Krassner saw the world. I read every issue, and I was astounded when he took on the unthinkable—the death of Kennedy. William Manchester had written a best-seller called *The Death of a President,* and Jackie Kennedy fought the book's publication until certain passages were removed. *The Realist* claimed to have gotten ahold of those sections, and printed them in one of its issues.

You have to realize that at this point in time, President Kennedy was still considered a secular figure of almost religious importance. His death was considered sacred. The concept of any type of humor that would directly involve this national nightmare was impossible to fathom.

Now, I must warn you, we are about to cross over a line here that will definitely separate a lot of us. There will be those of you who will read the following and close this book and toss it in the trash, while others will not be able to put it down. We've come to a bridge a lot of you might not want to cross. It's one of the first bridges I crossed that took me to where I am today. I am not doing this to shock anyone. Nor am I interested in having young teens flip out. I read this stuff when I was sixteen. It didn't damage me in the least. If anything, this was my baptism in the healing power of laughter. If my sense of humor had a bar mitzvah, this was it.

An excerpt from *The Parts Left Out of the Kennedy Book*

by Paul Krassner, 1967

American leaders tend to have schizophrenic approaches toward one another. They want to expose each other's human frailties at the same time that they do *not* want to remove their fellow emperors' clothes. Bobby

Kennedy privately abhors Lyndon Johnson, but publicly calls him "great, and I mean that in every sense of the word." Johnson has referred to Bobby as "that little shit" in private, but continues to laud him for the media.

Gore Vidal has no such restraint. On a television program in London, he explained why Jacqueline Kennedy will never relate to Lyndon Johnson. During that tense flight from Dallas to Washington after the assassination, she inadvertently walked in on Johnson as he was standing over the casket of his predecessor and chuckling. This disclosure was the talk of London, but did not reach these shores.

Of course, President Johnson is often given to inappropriate responses—witness the puzzled timing of his smile when he speaks of grave matters—but we must also assume that Mrs. Kennedy had been traumatized that day and her perception was likely to have been colored by the tragedy. This state of shock must have underlain an incident on Air Force One that this writer conceives to be delirium, but which Mrs. Kennedy insists she actually saw.

"I'm telling you this for the historical record," she said, "so that people a hundred years from now will know what I had to go through."

She corroborated Gore Vidal's story about Lyndon Johnson, continuing: "That man was crouching over the corpse, no longer chuckling but breathing hard and moving his body rhythmically. At first I thought he must be performing some mysterious symbolic rite he'd learned from Mexicans or Indians as a boy. And then I realized—there is only one way to say this—he was literally fucking my husband in the throat. In the bullet wound in the front of his throat. He reached a climax and dismounted. I froze. The next thing I remember, he was being sworn in as the new President."

[Handwritten marginal notes: 1. Check with Rankin—did secret autopsy show semen in throat wound? 2. Is this simply necrophilia or was LBJ trying to change entry wound from grassy knoll into exit wound from Book Depository by enlarging it?]

The glaze lifted from Jacqueline Kennedy's eyes.

"I don't believe that Lyndon Johnson had anything to do with a conspiracy, but I do know this—my husband taught me about the nuances of power—if Jack were miraculously to come back to life and suddenly appear in front of Johnson, the first thing Johnson would do now is kill him." She smiled sardonically, adding, "Unless Bobby beat him to it."

• • •

Now there's an eye-opener for you, a jalapeño for the soul, if you will. And now more than forty years after the fact, it still bangs around in my head—much like the bullet supposedly did in the car that fateful day. Imagine my surprise when I read that passage at the age of sixteen . . . so much for Camelot!

I have never laughed like that before; nor have I very often since. It brought my nervous system to a halt, as if I were hit by a stun gun. My breath was caught in my throat. Then somehow, against all sense of the values and decency instilled in me, I expelled a laugh of epic proportions. It was a laugh full of screaming and tears. It was as if someone were scratching their nails on a blackboard with one hand and tickling me with the other.

I knew I shouldn't be laughing, but I was and it felt good. It unraveled a psychic knot of pain that had been tied up in me ever since that scratchy announcement came over the speaker system in my high school. It shook me to my roots. I had crossed the border into a foreign and forbidden land where I didn't understand the language or the customs, but I felt better there.

There are, no doubt, millions of people who would consider my laughter at this very dirty, absolutely filthy joke my ticket to eternal damnation. Obviously I'm not one of them. And there isn't much middle ground here. Either Mr. Krassner made you laugh or he shocked you into utter silence.

I can sense some of you thinking, *Well, that's enough of his nonsense; I have better things to do with my time.* And you'd be right, of course, but only for yourself. That's what separates us and why we find each other so strange. So, to you I say good-bye. As for the few of you left on my somewhat skewed side, read on.

GENERAL RULES OF HEALTH

A doctor puts a rectal thermometer in his top pocket, as if it were an appeal to a higher authority.

One of the biggest problems facing this country today is our obsession with our health—even when there is nothing wrong with us. We stress over our health so much it actually makes us sick. Which is one of the reasons we need national health care. But that's a totally different story.

The mixed messages we receive on an almost daily basis don't help. Every time doctors tell us something is good for us, ten years later they tell us it's bad. Then they tell us it's good again. Case in point: eggs.

When I was a kid, we had a pyramid of food, and eggs were always at the top of the fucking pyramid. They were the best things ever. You could be stranded in a desert with only eggs to eat and you could live forever. If you could have lain your own eggs, you would have been king of the town. "Man, oh man," we used to say, "thank God for the hen."

Then something strange happened. The country was on code orange over eggs. "Emergency! Emergency! Drop the eggs. They must be destroyed." Why? Because some guys in white coats discovered that eggs contain cholesterol, and, they told us, cholesterol is evil. On the what's-more-evil chart, there was Hitler and then there was cholesterol. It should be noted that depending on who conducted the survey, however, the order could be reversed. Still, it was clear that whether eggs were in the number one or the number two position, they weren't a good thing.

So, many of us stopped eating eggs. And guess what? Fifteen years after the Ban the Egg campaign, the same scientists went, "Son of a bitch! Eggs are good! Let's dance." Eggs are good? Really? But what about the cholesterol?

This is when we found out that there are two types of cholesterol. There's good cholesterol and bad cholesterol. And you know what occurred to me at the time? *Bullshit!* I was supposed to believe that one cholesterol wears a white hat and the other wears a black hat, and they go around in our systems and have a shoot-out. Unbelievable.

But here's an interesting fact. In the time period that people stopped eating eggs there was an epidemic of a disease called macular degeneration, which makes people lose their sight. Apparently the doctors on the no-egg bandwagon didn't realize that you need eggs to see shit! Brilliant.

Now, of course not everyone got macular degeneration from not eating eggs. The reason for that—and this is what the doctors have always seemed to forget—is that everybody's health in this world is totally different. What's good for one of you could kill the person sitting next to you right now. My health, your health, everybody's health is unique.

In short, we are all like snowflakes. Medically speaking, we are beautiful, no-two-are-alike works of art. When thrown together, however, we eventually become slush—filthy, disgusting puddles of thick gray water that can ruin both your shoes and your life. That said, in my vast experience and after years of painstaking research, I have concluded that there are only two general rules of health that actually pertain to everybody.

The first is that the good die young but pricks live forever. John F. Kennedy and Strom Thurmond immediately come to mind, but feel free to insert your own family members in there. Anyway, in order to ensure your longevity, follow this simple plan: Pick out a kid who lives nearby, and every time you see him on the street, run outside and scream, "Get out of here, you little shit!" Trust me on this. It's better than taking vitamins.

The second rule is a bit more complicated and takes some real dedication to carry out. And that is, if you masturbate twenty times a day, you will never make it out of your front door. You might be able to make it to the door, but when you try to squeeze the handle, you'll pass out. I know this because before I was on TV, I supervised this very study at the renowned Lewis Black Research Center. It was all very official—the study was conducted while I was wearing a standard-issue lab coat complete with a rectal thermometer in the breast pocket. Let me assure you, these results are written in stone. I ran the same test three days in a row, and there was never a deviation. Science can be very, very messy, but it's also very, very important.

I should note at this time that the above results are merely for men. Women, I believe, have a higher threshold for enjoyment, and their masturbation-to-pass-out ratio is thirty to one. Granted, this is all conjecture as I have not been able to get any female volunteers to agree to come to my lab. The quest for truth, therefore, goes on. Look for the results in the next book.

VIRAL INFECTIONS

There's a daytime NyQuil and a nighttime NyQuil—take whichever one you want; your infection doesn't care what time it is.

There's a health concern that was big news a while ago but we stupidly thought it went away. Forever. And why did we think it went away? Because the government told us it did. But guess what? It seems there's still a possibility there may be a smallpox epidemic in this country.

That's right, smallpox. An epidemic. A smallpox epidemic! How could this be? Well, it's really quite simple. It seems the smallpox vaccine that we were given, the one we were told was going to last forever, actually had a shelf life. Yep, it wore off!

Now, a vaccine that expires sounds like pretty big news, doesn't it? The kind you'd probably want to share immediately. Well, our government didn't tell us until there was a possibility of emergency conditions. What a crackerjack group of fuckers! How could they not call us?

"Hey, Lew, your smallpox vaccine has worn off. You want another?"

Um, let me think. Yeah, you're fucking right I want another because, until now, my whole life has been a delusion. Every day I would wake up and say, "It's gonna suck today, but at least I won't get smallpox."

Here's how long it took the government to tell us about this concern. Imagine going to a public bathroom only to flush the toilet and have the toilet water hit you in the face. Then, as you walk out of the bathroom, you see a big sign on the back of the door that reads WARNING, TOILET WATER MAY HIT YOU IN THE FACE. But that's how things work in this country. We get our government-issued goggles only after diluted piss stings our eyes.

Well, I'm not taking this lying down. If I get smallpox, I'll file suit against the federal government because they took me out of a very important class to administer that vaccine. And maybe if I had taken that class, I wouldn't have to be yelling at eighty drunks at two in the morning for a living. I could have had a real job where I could be drunk by two in the afternoon. The government owes me big-time.

But the smallpox scare wasn't the only time the U.S. government misled us, medically speaking, anyway. That was an isolated incident. Every other year they issue a more traditional warning: "Get a flu shot! Get a flu shot! This is gonna be the worst flu ever, and it's coming our way!"

It was a warning that I usually ignored. What, I figured, do I need a flu shot for? I'm relatively young, I'm in good health, I'm not in a high-risk group—I'll take my chances. And guess what? In all of those years, I never got the flu. Not once.

Last year, however, the anxiety over getting the flu shot reached a fever pitch across the country because there just wasn't enough vaccine to go around. And for the first time I could remember in ten or twelve years, every government health organization worked overtime to assure us that if your general health was good, if you were relatively young and you weren't in a high-risk group, you really didn't need a flu shot. "Don't sweat it," they insisted. That's when I became determined to get a goddamn flu shot!

Obviously, considering the government's history of lying to us, I was convinced this really was going to be the worst flu ever, and I, for one, was not dying of some pissant viral infection. And I got very lucky. Unlike all those senior citizens lined up in Florida, I think I scored perhaps the very last flu shot to be given in New York City.

Screw that eighty-three-year-old who was taking his damn sweet time maneuvering his walker up the steps to the clinic. When I *accidentally* knocked him to the side I wasn't being mean, just pragmatic—I was younger and there was still so much more for me to give. I wasn't thinking of myself, which is one of my biggest faults. I've always been about giving back. Who's your daddy now, you selfish old prick?

Anyway, the shot was mine and, as advertised, I never did get the flu. I did, however, get a cold that lasted for nine weeks. Now, don't get me wrong, I'm not complaining. I like having colds because I get to take my favorite drug—NyQuil. Forget that other sissy-ass crap. Give me the NyQuil. It's like 180-proof and, as far as I'm concerned, it's the over-the-counter moonshine of medicine.

When I get a cold, I want something that will totally screw me up and make the constant blur seem a little more interesting. And NyQuil even comes with choices. You can get it in either red or green, and, it should be noted, they are the only substances on the planet that actually taste like red and green. Still, it's a festive cure-all. Red and green, after all, are the colors of Christmas, and let me tell you, that stuff makes one dandy eggnog.

Here's what you can toast to this year with that eggnog. When autumn comes around again, the government will start their familiar refrain: "Get a flu shot! Get a flu shot! This is going to be the worst flu ever, and it's coming our way!" The odds are, they eventually have to be right. And I already know how it will happen. Some guy who didn't wipe himself properly is going to get on a crappy little boat in Formosa and head our way. When he gets here, he'll be so excited to be in the States he'll shake everybody's hand and then . . . *boom!* We're all going to get the flu.

At least I'll be ready. I'm stocking up on NyQuil as we speak. And nobody better get in my way.

POLITICS AND PROMS

It's all about the balloons.

Being born and raised around the capital of the nation had a rather profound effect on me. My local news was national news. The federal government was always in my face, and everyone around me worked for the government.

I even participated in two campaigns, which meant I was that kid who handed out the buttons or the boxes of bad fried chicken. And that was all it took for me to realize I wouldn't be running for public office. It was hard enough keeping myself inspired, let alone having to inspire total strangers.

Since I was so excellent at handing out crap, I was rewarded with a trip to Atlantic City in 1964 for a visit to the Democratic National Convention. They brought the youth of America in for an afternoon of inspirational speeches, which told us nothing we hadn't heard a thousand times before. The event left me profoundly depressed about the state of our democracy. The highlight was supposedly shaking hands with the president's daughters, Luci Baines and Lynda Bird Johnson. *Wow,* I thought, *they are even uglier in person.*

As I write this, Laura Bush is speaking at the Republican National Convention. I don't know when it

became imperative for the wives of candidates to speak at conventions, but it sure makes the whole thing seem like high school to me. Not that the wife shouldn't speak, but it's never been that important for me to hear what she has to say. What's she going to reveal that we don't already know? "Here's a little secret, he's really kind of a prick with low self-esteem. That whole tough guy image is just overcompensation."

And in the name of all that is holy, can we keep the kids from opening their yaps? What kind of guy wants to be president so much that he exposes his kids to public ridicule on that level? It's abusive. It turns it all into a very bad pep rally. Can't we all just grow up at some point and be adult about this? We are electing a leader, not casting a television series. "I really like *him,* but that wife of his just won't do for network television."

Politics hasn't changed much since high school, except instead of a wife, in high school there was a campaign manager who makes the speech and tells everyone just how great a guy the candidate is. Personally, I got the biggest kick out of writing the speeches for student body elections. Since there really wasn't that much someone could do if elected, it left a lot of room for writing jokes and generally making fun of the whole process. It was an excellent outlet for my growing sense of sarcasm.

During my senior year I helped write most of the speeches for the candidates and their managers. I was writing for people running against each other and nobody seemed to mind. At the time it didn't strike any of us as the least bit strange. We just wanted it to be entertaining. And that's a big part of what politics is supposed to be now, only they don't know what fun is, which is one of many reasons I got tired of it. The way I see it is, if it's not going to be more mature, it should at least be more entertaining.

I was chairman of our junior prom committee—now *that's* something for the résumé. Imagine, I was in charge of a prom and nobody thought I was gay. Well, in truth, we didn't really know there were gays back then. Sure, there was one guy, but we just thought he was strange. My friends and I were, by now, running the student government; not because we were geniuses—it was mostly because no one else wanted to.

And I wanted to run the junior prom to make sure we didn't spend any money on it. I figured the senior prom was what mattered so we should use the junior prom as a fund-raiser. If a girl had been put in charge, she would have wanted the evening to be special and would have spent too much money making sure it was. I was going bare bones on the whole thing. We called it "Showboat," God knows why, and gave it a Southern theme. I figured, keep the lights low, throw in a little magnolia and moonlight, and voilà, a Wal-Mart prom.

So I picked up some red brick contact paper and slapped it on the gym seats, and then, with my friend Charley, went to find something to slap on the bricks. Honeysuckle was in bloom, which seemed perfect, and we brought back pounds of it. Actually, it turned out to be pounds of honeysuckle and poison ivy. A number of my fellow students spent a lot of time leaning against the gym seats and ended up bearing the brunt of my frugality. Lesson number sixty-five: You get what you pay for.

I went to both proms, with different girls. Each of my dates had started going out with me a few weeks before the prom and broke up with me a few weeks after. Coincidence? I think not.

MUSIC

"'Scuse me while I kiss the sky."
—Jimi Hendrix

When I was fourteen, I got an Emerson 888 transistor radio for my birthday and I listened to it at night while I did my homework. As I spun through the stations, I found WABC New York and hope entered my life. Somehow in the ether of radio waves, I arrived at the doorstep of the world. There was something wonderful and mysterious that existed outside of the suburbs, or maybe just inside my head, and the music took me to places I had never imagined. There were sounds that could turn me right side up and upside down and will me with a passion I didn't know I had and a sadness I had never felt. It was music. It was my first drug. It was heaven.

There was Dion and the Belmonts and Buddy Holly and Elvis Presley and the Ronettes and the Shangri-Las—the list was endless. But it all burst open, as is more than well established, when the Beatles came to America and appeared on *The Ed Sullivan Show.* They sang "I Wanna Hold Your Hand." I will never understand it. I couldn't control myself. I was grinning like a John Edwards. They brought a joyous energy that overwhelmed me. For years they provided the soundtrack of my life. Even now I can hear a song of theirs and go back to that time and place.

Then came the Rolling Stones, and they were like the flip side of the coin. They were the bad boys. I went to their first American concert and it was the first rock show I had ever seen. I saw Mick Jagger dance and I thought, *If he can dance, so can I.*

Of course, all that has changed since the advent of MTV. (Or as I like to call it, the boner network.) These days music is available to every kid everywhere. Now the little bastards come home from school and they go, "Mom, I'm going to watch MTV." Then they go up to their rooms and lock their doors and they put their peckers right up on the set and wait for liftoff. When I was growing up, we had to flip the pages of *National Geographic* magazine really fast in order to achieve the same result— "Oh my God! Oh my God! She's moving!"

Still, the more things change, the more they stay the same. Music still provides you with a vision—a vision, you'll find, that changes over time. For instance, let's say you fall in love. Well, every time you hear a particular song, you'll think of the woman you were in love with. The first time you hear it, perhaps you'll see her running through a field of clover. And then the second time you hear it, she'll be taking a milk bath with a loofah. (What can I say, I happen to think a milk bath is a nice idea, and a loofah makes it a better one.) Then, after a few years go by, you have a horrible breakup and you find yourself sitting at a bar late at night, having that last shot of Jägermeister before you hit the road, and something familiar will come on the jukebox. And despite the fact that she broke up with you a year ago, you'll hear that song again and you'll still see her in your mind . . . this time standing on a cliff being torn apart by coyotes.

And that's what music's really all about. That's the wonder of it. That's the joy of it.

(MIS)GUIDANCE COUNSELOR

There is a record, and it follows you around for the rest of your life.

I was the top male student in my high school, and there were more than five hundred students in my graduating class. I am not telling you this to impress you. It's just that it's an integral part of this next story. Besides, I had become really good at getting good grades—a skill you can learn without learning anything else at the same time. I had successfully learned to play the game.

It was my senior year, and I knew I wanted to go to college, because I certainly wasn't ready to go out and get a job and I had no desire to be drafted. I wouldn't have responded very well to taking orders. And besides that, my mother wouldn't even let me be a Boy Scout. I had been a Cub Scout, and when that was over she said, "You are never putting on another uniform again." Plus I wasn't too keen on the idea of getting up at the crack of dawn to start shooting things.

So I took the SATs, which I did well on but not great except for math—I knocked that part out of the park. I was really good at math, but I had no use for it. I visited a number of schools but really hadn't had the vaguest idea what I was, or should be, looking for. I stumbled blindly into a number of places, based on where my friends were going. Unlike many of my friends, however, I was completely clueless as to how to make a choice about which college to go to.

On the upside, I knew what I didn't want. My father and I drove up to Hamilton College, at the time an all-male school completely isolated in upstate New York. *No women—how perfectly hellish,* I thought. My father thought it was great—at which point I told him to apply.

Granted, we had guidance counselors in our high school, but they didn't really seem to know how to live up to their job titles. We'd have been better off with a Hopi holy man in a mud hut somewhere. So I finally applied to Yale, Princeton, Brown, Amherst, Williams, and Georgetown. Take a good look at that list and let's continue. It might have helped if I had known at the time what I wanted to specialize in, but at that point I had not idea at all. Except for sex. Since I wasn't getting lucky in high school, I knew I wanted to have sex in college. It's important to have a goal, and that was mine.

I just figured I could go to a good school a with lot of stuff to choose from, and it would all fall into place. I showed my guidance counselor the list of schools I was applying to and he said they seemed like excellent choices. No kidding. He said I would definitely get in to Williams, Amherst, and Georgetown, and went on to say that Brown, Yale, and Princeton would be tougher but certainly in the range of probability.

I was the top male in my class academically. I had done all sorts of activities. I had put together the junior prom and the senior trip. I was on our donkey basketball team. If there had been a lacrosse team, I would have been on that too.

What he neglected to tell me was that there were tons of us little baby boomers applying to schools and, as a result, competition was fierce. He also failed to mention that my SAT scores weren't as strong as they should be and that I really had to be sure I got interviewed everywhere to have a fighting chance. Oh well, he was a very busy man. And, to be fair, back then applying to colleges hadn't become a full-time job and an industry in and of itself like it is today. I guess thousands of disappointed baby boomers wanted to make sure their kids weren't going to get screwed, not like they did.

Anyway, I ripped open the letters I received from each school with eager anticipation, fully expecting to receive nothing but good news. Every school except Georgetown rejected me. I felt like shit. Much like the Olympic athlete who devotes four years to training and then ends up just shy of the bronze, in fourth place. I felt as if I had failed. That all of this time I put in had truly been for naught. I may not have known where I wanted to go or why, but I sure wanted to get in. I wanted to cross the finish line. And I certainly wanted to bat better than one for six.

Sure, I got into Georgetown, but by then I had realized I didn't want to go there anymore. It was too close to my home, and the one thing I had finally realized about college was that I wanted to go to a place where my parents couldn't get to me on weekends. Besides, the only reason I had applied there was because it had a good foreign service school, but I was no longer interested in the foreign service. Too much stuff to learn, and all that time around D.C. had killed my taste for working for the government.

This is the kind of moment when people will tell you

TYPICAL SENIOR CLASS COUNCIL MINUTES

The meeting was called to order at 2:45 P.M. by our leader of divine providence, Don Smith.

The Treasurer Phil Olsen was the only member not present.

Don Smith reported that there is only 37¢ in the treasury.

Old Business

Ken Beard showed the films of the Senior Class Picnic. It was an excellent 45 feet of the 45 Seniors present--a foot apiece. It was just great.

Committee Reports

Grover Zucker gave his report on the talent show and Doris Mills gave her report on the talent show and as it appears now this year for the first time there will be two talent shows.

Lewis Black, class trip chairman, reported that this year's trip will be held in the school gym with slides being shown of New York City. The trip's cost will be $34 to cover the cost of chaperones and janitorial services.

New Business

Nancy Mercogliano asked if the class would reimburse her 50¢ for 10 stamps she bought to mail out class business. Bitter debate arose over why she did not send picture postcards on which the postage is prepaid. Len Hughes asked why she couldn't use 4¢ stamps and was enlightened to the fact that they do not exist.

Lewis Black made a motion to amend the constitution to provide that all class council representatives be between the ages of 20 and 22. The motion was defeated, due mainly to Mark Harris' threats to burn his Senior Class membership card if the motion was passed.

The meeting was adjourned promptly at 6:03 P.M.

Congratulations to Missy Shepherd for winning the Miss Silver Spring contest.

Special thanks to Lewis Black for his long hours and many (remember quantity is more important than quality) contributions.

And we are waiting for: "How can people of the major religious traditions of our country contribute to the unity and purpose of our nation?" as a Hollywood spectacular.

that things happen for a reason. Well, the reason this happened is because I trusted my guidance counselor to give good guidance. He didn't. Sure, he may just have been the instrument fate used to change the course of my life, but that was of no solace. And let's face it; the man screwed up big time. Authority was no longer infallible in my eyes, and the next time I wouldn't be so trusting.

My counselor couldn't apologize enough, but that was of no help at all. He set up interviews with dozens of schools that couldn't believe I was still available. Nice, but now I was wary of anyone who really wanted me. How good a school could it be if they were willing to put up with me? Many were small, midwestern colleges, miles from any form of civilization, and the black-and-white pictures in the school brochures of young coeds in dowdy pleated skirts did little to pique my interest.

The only good news was that by that time I knew what I wanted from a school: It had to have a drama department. You see, that spring we'd had a talent show, and my friends and I had written the book for it, giving the show its through line. I played a talent agent for whom all of the acts performed to see if they could get on the prestigious *Ed Sullivan Show.* And breaking with the traditional format of "Gee, weren't the kids just wonderful? Those Ukrainian folk dances were sure special," I told them they just weren't that good. It made for very good comedy and was a huge success. I was hooked. I didn't think I would ever pursue theater as a career, but I wanted to at least give it a try. So I decided I would spend a year at the University of Maryland and then find a school where I could pursue my dream.

Brimstone Brief

Lewis Black Plans A Career In Drama

Lewis Black needs little introduction to Springbrook students. He is well-known throughout the school for his scholastic achievements, his willingness to work, and his witty personality.

As a member of the Class of '66, Lewis has contributed much of his time and effort to his fellow classmates.

Directly involved in the formation of the class government, Lewis was chairman of the Activities of 9th grade. Following this, he went on to become chairman of the Student Education Committee as a sophomore, and chairman of the Junior Prom Committee in 11th grade. This year Lewis is chairman of the Senior Class Trip Committee as well as a writer for the VERIST, the Senior Class newspaper.

Because of his interest and ability in the field of dramatics, Lewis volunteered to co-write the script of the 1966 Talent Show.

With plans to enter Georgetown University's School of Arts and Sciences in the fall, Lewis has successfully maintained a superior scholastic average. Rated as third in the senior class, he has been awarded a Springbrook letter for his scholastic achievements and also a National Merit Letter of Commendation. Last spring, Lewis received the additional honor of being inducted into the Springbrook chapter of the National Honor Society.

Speaking about his future plans, Lewis said, "I wish to go into Dramatics because I find it the most exciting field. I don't wish to study acting, (I can't) but the playwriting side of it. I'd like to end up as a playwright or drama critic.

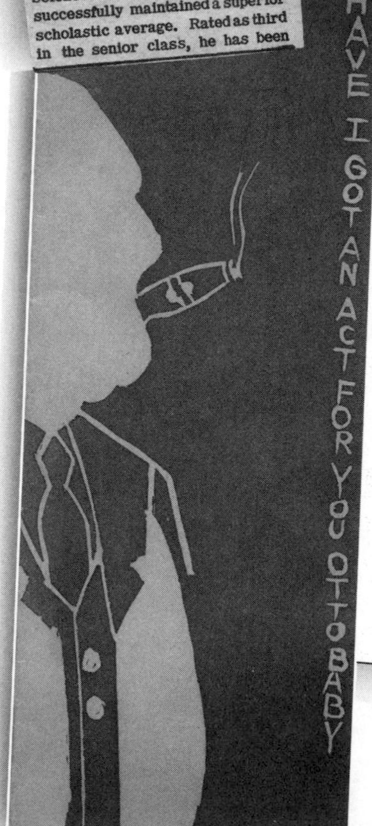

Class of 1966

Commencement

Friday, June 17, 1966

6:30 P. M.

THE POST OFFICE

Fuck you, Ben Franklin.

Less than forty-eight hours after graduating high school, I went to work the night shift at the Silver Spring post office, from eleven o'clock at night until eight in the morning. There's a transition for you. I now had a clear understanding of the term "culture shock." I may as well have moved from Silver Spring to Bhutan because the post office is another world, with its own rules, especially on the night shift. Let me put it this way: If the post office didn't already exist, Kafka would have invented it. And working for the post office is exactly how you might envision it, only worse.

My job there was quite simple. I would grab the mail sacks that the trucks dropped off like clockwork, dump them out, and then box the letters so that they could be sorted. Contributing to the tedium of it all, the din of the sorting machines would provide an endless sound track for the night. And if you listened closely, you could discern the unspoken lyrics "I hate my life, I hate my life" droning on, over and over and over like a song without end.

There was, however, an upside to working at night—it paid a little more money. But there was also a downside—the night shift attracts a certain type of person, to put it diplomatically. For instance, I had a conversation with one of my coworkers on my first night as a government employee that I will never, ever forget. I've desperately tried to forget it, but unfortunately, it is permanently burned into my mind.

It went like this. At one point—and don't ask me how we got to this point, there was nothing that led up to it—he asked if I knew what a plate job was.

"Uhhhhm, no, I don't," was my reply.

He then told me. And there's no reason any of you should know this, no reason I should tell you, except to give you an idea of the world that I had entered. A plate job is when a woman sits over a pane of glass held by a man, who is lying down on the floor. She then takes a dump on the glass, preferably when it's positioned over his face.

Well, the neurons in my brain just exploded. "Huh? Why? Where? How? Are you kidding me? A what to whom and why for? And that makes someone . . . happy?"

Jesus, I was not prepared for this type of nightly conversation. So I responded as any sane eighteen-year-old would. I excused myself, walked over to a cigarette machine, and bought a pack of cigarettes. I then went outside, lit up, and truly smoked a cigarette for the first time in my life. Okay, I had smoked cigarettes before, but this time I was inhaling—really inhaling, in hopes of choking my mind with smoke in an effort to rid it of the smell of that lady's dump. The worst thing was, I had none of the problems people have when they first start smoking. I liked it—probably because I was going to need a friend if I was going to be locked up with these psychopaths for the next few months.

I smoked half a pack without any noticeable ill effects. I had moved from an idyllic high school life to the third rung of hell, and I responded maturely by finding something that would allow me to kill myself slowly. The plan, however, was not foolproof—I was still alive at the end of the summer.

I have never had a worse job. Even when I spent one summer cleaning out a refrigerator for a vending machine company where the smell of sour milk hung in the cold air around me. Or even when I helped build a new blacktop driveway in the heat of the summer sun. Those were cakewalks compared to the post office. The mail never stopped. It never, ever stopped. It came in wave after wave. In gray sacks, with the words "US MAIL" printed in bold black letters. It came in letters and boxes of all shapes and sizes. There was always more—never an end in sight.

It made me crazy. I didn't have a good night's sleep that summer. I would wake up and my pillows had become gray sacks and I had to beat them with my fists to turn them back into pillows. I began to wish that a mail truck would wreck so that there would be an end to this madness.

Since then, whenever I read of postal employees going ballistic and firing off round after round of ammunition, I fully understand their pain. They just want the mail to stop, even if it takes a few deaths to do it. Horrible, I know, but unless you have stood under those fluorescent lights staring at an endless sea of mail, you will never really comprehend what is going on in their heads.

I was lucky. The guys on my watch never took their frustrations out on other human beings. They were rather evolved. They merely shot at the rats in the parking lot.

THE UNIVERSITY OF MARYLAND

The terrapin was the mascot. Need I say more?

I spent my freshman year at the University of Maryland. I was living at home, while many of my friends went out of state, bringing back enviable tales of adventure, drugs, and romance. Since I was living with my parents, there was no adventure, there were no drugs to speak of, and any romance was, unfortunately, a decidedly solitary affair. There was, however, weight gain. At least I had that going for me.

I was lucky that a few of my friends—Cliff, Lenny, and Don—went to the university with me. Without having them around, I would have completely flipped out. Not a day went by that I didn't dream of killing my high school guidance counselor. I was *thisclose* to inspiring the kind of headlines usually reserved for people with three names—people like John Wayne Gacy and Mark David Chapman. "Student Lewis Niles Black Sought in Gruesome Death of Counselor; Police Find Brilliant Essay."

If we hadn't been born and raised in Maryland and if we had been immensely talented musicians raised in Liverpool, we would have been the Beatles. Cliff is about as smart as they come. He became one of the guys who helped create the Internet. He had a great laugh and a

Better bathroom scriptures 7/16/67

Sir:

What is wrong with the University?

It is not the University's impersonality or the abundance of large lectures. Nor is it the University's overabundance of virgins. What is basically wrong at our school is the lack of good literature on the walls of the men's lavatories. These scribblings don't even make it worthwhile to go to the bathroom.

The lavatory walls are completely covered with filth. Even the artwork is poor. I would even go as far to say that it is below high school standard. It just lacks class.

My first visit to one of the University lavatories was taken in the hope that I would find there, great words of wisdom. I felt these lavatories would be something I could point to with pride. But I was appalled by the sheer smut for smut's sake. Now I'm not being prudish - funny, intellectual smut is good. (Take "Candy" for example) Plain garbage tends to make monotonous reading material. I feel that this school's creative minds with just a little time and effort can produce excellent lavatory literature.

At the moment what do we have that compares with the immortal bathroom note - "God isn't dead-He just doesn't want to get involved?" What can the University match it with except pure, hardcore pornography. Certainly someone who takes Econ. 197 can produce something better than - Call Jane - 243-0146-38-22-34.

It is my hope that there will emerge a rebellious group of underground lavatory scribblers, who will bring to the University a golden age in bathroom scriptures.

Lewis Black

better smile. He would have been George. Lenny was a blue-collar kid with real intelligence, the kind of guy who can cripple you with his wit. He would have been Ringo. And Don was the one who thought before he spoke. He would have been Paul. I would have liked to have been John, but I wasn't really. Maybe that's why we never became the Beatles. We were all living at home, and if we hadn't had one another, we would have killed ourselves.

The guys and I spent most of our time in the commuter lounge, sucking on smokes and drinking coffee. When that exotic location proved too mundane, we would try to stave off our ennui in the library looking up books with titles like *Wound Ballistics.* We also did doctorate-level research on a variety of genital abnormalities out of boredom. I mostly took classes that I had already taken in high school. My mission was to get the best grades possible so I could transfer to another, much better school.

Here's how bad things had gotten. The highlights of the year were the times we would head to a rock club to listen to a group called the Great Dames. The band consisted of four very beautiful, very tall women who would transport me out of my ever-present depression. Sadly, they were nearly the sum total of my sex life. I never had the nerve to speak to any of them; I would just constantly fantasize about our lives together. It's amazing how little it takes to keep a man going.

That fall, on the advice of my prom date's mom (like I said, things were really bad!), I visited the University of North Carolina at Chapel Hill. My plan was to take a quick look at the school and then go over to Duke University, where I thought I would apply for admission. I walked onto the campus of UNC, however, and that was all it took. It is as close as I had ever been to being in love at first sight. The place was absolutely beautiful.

I have never been a big nature person, and, having worn glasses most of my life, I have never had much of a visual aesthetic. Still, I was absolutely overwhelmed by how serenely pretty it was. I had found the ideal campus for me. I decided at that moment that this was where I wanted to go to school. I felt like I was home—a wonderful home where my parents didn't live, a home where there was adventure and drugs and sex. Oh, God, I wanted a home filled with sex. I was sure I had found my Xanadu.

EUROPE

Thank God for Europe. Without it, a lot us wouldn't know where we came from.

Between working nights at the post office over the summer and living at home during my first year of college, I was able to put together enough money to spend part of the next summer in Europe. I planned to hitchhike and get laid and hitchhike and get laid and get laid and get laid. Such is the grandiose imagination of fevered youth. So with my friend Cliff, I packed up for a tour of the continent. It was a great time to be young, because you could actually travel for five dollars a day.

The first stop was London. On our first night there, we managed to stumble onto some sort of a stripper/hooker joint. As we wandered aimlessly through Soho, we heard a young woman calling from a doorway, "You boys looking for fun?" Fun? Did she say fun? Absolutely. We were in desperate search of fun. And now we knew there was a God.

We followed her down the stairs. She was stunning, an absolute knockout for sure. Well, she was a woman and she was talking to us. Another woman greeted us and took Cliff to one booth, and my vision of loveliness took me to another.

We were now officially dead meat. Together, we had enough brains to extricate ourselves before we ran through our meager bankroll, but separated, we were now idiots. According to the woman who took me to the booth, if I bought her enough drinks I could then watch her strip, and if I had a lot more money, I could take her back to my hotel.

"Don't you want to buy me a drink?" she purred, speaking directly to my genitals.

My head was swimming. *Jesus,* I thought, *I can't afford this. I'll never make it to Paris at this rate.* But, of course, I said, "Yes, yes, yes, whatever you want, it's on me."

One drink couldn't hurt and then I would go back to my room and not spend any money for the next two days. They brought over a bad bit of the bubbly. And as my genitals sank into a depression, my mind went into a total panic. I was in way over my head—I knew it, and she no doubt knew it too. I began to babble.

"You see, we just got over here today and we really don't know what we are doing and we really don't have the kind of money needed to really have some fun and if we have some fun we'll run through our money and have to go home. We never should have left America. I am really sorry about this."

My first moment with a hooker and I had a breakdown. She left me there, staring at the empty glasses. I looked over at my friend Cliff. He had three glasses on the table. *Jesus,* I thought, *he's going for it.* He doesn't care. He won't have enough money to get home. He'll live in London for the rest of his life. Wow, what guts. And then the woman sitting with him got up and left the room. Cliff raced over to me. "Jesus, let's get the hell out of here." We raced back into the London night. He hadn't meant to buy the drinks. It was all a horrible mistake. So much for getting laid; maybe we'd do better with the hitchhiking.

Next it was on to Paris, where we managed to get separated on the metro. I stepped off the train, but he was stuck. And we didn't have a hotel yet. So for the next few hours, as if we were in a bad slapstick comedy, we kept missing each other. It didn't help that I knew not one word of the French language. Finally, by a stroke of dumb luck, we managed to stumble into each other.

By the time we got to the cheapest digs we could find, I had an overwhelming need to use the bathroom. But there wasn't one in the room or on the floor. We had a sink and an apparatus that looked like a toilet without a seat and that had hot and cold running water and a metal stopper in the drain. We stared at it. *What the hell is that?* I wondered. The manager came up to assist us in our search for the bathroom or water closet or WC or whatever the hell they called the place where they did their business. Cliff spoke French, but no matter how he put it, the guy just kept pointing to this contraption that looked like a sink that hadn't grown up.

"That can't be it," I cried.

"He said that's it."

And so Cliff left the room as I squatted over what I would learn later is known as a bidet, a device used to bathe one's genitals. Despite having graduated third in my class, I had to travel all the way to Paris to learn one of life's most important lessons—one doesn't shit in the bidet because one has to clean it up. It's an awful introduction to the City of Love. When we left the hotel to sightsee, we passed the open door of a real bathroom on the floor just below ours. And any doubts I'd had about the French disliking us were confirmed.

The only thing dumber than shitting in a bidet in Paris

is trying to hitchhike out of Paris. That was what we figured we'd do; everyone hitchhikes through Europe, don't they? Well, not us. . . .

Cliff and I were like the plague. We walked as far as we could in an oppressive heat before we realized that Paris is really huge and that we weren't going to make it at that rate and would have to take a train to Biarritz and then on to San Sebastian and, finally, to Pamplona for the running of the bulls . . . just like Hemingway.

We met our friend Ed in San Sebastian, which is an absolutely spectacular spot, especially if you have lived in the suburbs your whole life and have never seen, well, anything. As much as London and Paris were revelations to three kids from Silver Spring, San Sebastian was an extraordinary city with an unparalleled vista and enough drink to last us forever. We actually bought wineskins that the locals filled up with vino. Hungover the next day, we all took the bus to Pamplona, which is definitely not the way Hemingway did it.

Pamplona was my Woodstock. I had tried to go to the real Woodstock back in the States, but my mother stopped me as I was walking out the door.

"What do you think you're doing?" she asked.

"I'm going to Woodstock."

"What, are you crazy? We took you to Woodstock when you were a kid. You've already been there and you didn't like it—it wasn't even crowded." I almost believed her.

Pamplona was bedlam. We wandered the streets with misfits of every nationality, exchanging whatever we were drinking for whatever they were drinking. Everyone was everyone else's best friend.

We had nowhere to sleep as every hotel was booked

and we hadn't really thought that one out. So we fell asleep in some all-night coffee spot only to be awakened by two Spanish couples, dressed in formal wear, who desperately wanted to share some of their magnum of champagne.

It was surreal, but if "surrealer" is actually a word, it would get "surrealer" just a couple of hours later, when the Catholic Church rolled out a big hoop-dee-doo ceremony and blessed all the alcoholics in sight.

This was the prelude to the running of the bulls. And in my drunken stupor, I thought I just might give it a go. That is, until I took a good long look at the bulls in the pen and realized they were real bulls that weren't kidding around and didn't seem all that happy about their situation. I quickly decided they didn't need me to run with them.

My friend Ed had read more Hemingway than I had and actually did the deed. It was a move on his part that was simultaneously impressive and stupid. I mean, in the end, *The Sun Also Rises* is fiction. Do we really know if Hemingway actually ran with the bulls? He sure as hell couldn't have eaten in all the restaurants that have plaques bearing his name. Besides, the guy ended up killing himself. Is that something else one would want to emulate?

Cliff and I looked on from the sidelines. Watching a group of drunks racing down the streets of Pamplona in front of a bunch of angry bulls is a vision that borders on madness. Then the whole gang runs into the bullfighting stadium where a few bulls with padded horns are let loose, just to put the icing on the cake. No one was gored that day, but a few were whacked around in the corrida like a bunch of rag dolls. The PETA people would have wept. The bullfight season was now open. And let's just say, it's a spectator sport that you need to be drunk to enjoy.

I had been studying Spanish in high school and college, but I quickly realized that all you needed to do to really master a language is have a few drinks. That way, you feel that you have an absolute grasp of what you are saying and what is being said to you. I am surprised to this day that I didn't say something to get myself killed.

The next morning we hopped a train to Madrid, and then it was down to the Costa del Sol—and eventually on to Milan, Florence, Pisa, Rome, Naples, and Sicily. Our tiny suburban minds were exploding with the overwhelming sense of history that surrounded us.

There is a lot of old shit in Europe, and most of it is worth the price of admission. My personal favorite was the collection of saints' bones at the Vatican, each in their own heavy silver containers. There was also a footprint allegedly made by Christ that we saw along the way in Italy. Apparently he appeared to Paul somewhere and left his footprint. You've got to love those Catholics. They sure know how to keep a Jew entertained.

From Sicily we hopped a boat to Tunis, Tunisia, to meet up with my friend Ray, whose dad was working for the Agency for International Development. The Israeli Six-Day War had started the day before (or was it the Seven-Day War—either way, for a war it was really fast) and we were the only Americans on the boat. I have never felt more like a Jew in my life. I wondered at what point they would discover the heritage Ed and I shared and throw us overboard. By the time we arrived in Tunis, which held the largest Jewish population in the Arab world outside of Israel, we discovered that every Jew had fled. Now, apparently, it was just Ed and I. And since neither of us was very Jewish, we would have denied it had they come around for a head count.

We spent most of our time there lounging around at the beach or shopping for trinkets to take home. Feeling obligated to get a feel for the culture, we found ourselves at an Arab music festival a few hours from Tunis. The audience was nothing but guys; apparently women have to listen to this stuff at home. Three hours later we still had no feel for the culture, and even less interest in Arab music. The highlight was a belly dancer, who seemed to really get the guys going through some sort of sexual innuendo that was completely alien to us. I have never seen men get that excited over a woman who had her clothes on.

After a few weeks of living like only Americans can in a third-world country—and by that I mean living a life with servants and a variety of wondrous foods served three times a day—we then took a boat to Marseilles before Cliff and I went on to Munich. Among other places, we visited the beer hall where Hitler had worked his magic years before. I was lucky enough to catch a drunken elderly German actually shouting, "Heil Hitler!" in the bathroom. And let me tell you, an experience like that makes for one bashful kidney.

But that incident wasn't the only reason I found Germany a bit strange. The Germans love to wear uniforms. Everyone seemed to have one. It sure made this Jew a little jumpy. We also visited Dachau. Having watched all those videos as a kid, it just seemed right to see it in person. Man, you wouldn't have known what went on there unless you paid really close attention. It was all rather spiffy, like some delightful holiday camp. The only thing that gave a clue to the horror that occurred there was a sign that read CREMATORIUM. It, mercifully, was closed.

We made our way by late-night bus to Berlin, which meant a long drive through East Berlin. Every few hours the East German police, who couldn't have studied our passports more carefully, stopped us. I kept wondering, *What if this is it?* They could just drag Cliff and me off the bus and keep us at one of their slave labor camps. And no one would be the wiser. It was dark, and the East German police were creepy even in daylight.

But that didn't stop me from visiting East Berlin. Crossing through the menacing wall, I reached the drabbest city I have ever seen. It was as if all possibility of color had been bleached out of the buildings. I have never been to a more depressing place; a few coats of paint alone would have helped.

I stayed long enough to go to the Berliner Ensemble, the theater company and stage where Bertolt Brecht worked. Many of you may not know who he is, but he wrote the musical classic *Threepenny Opera,* featuring the song "The Ballad of Mack the Knife." Devote yourself to a life in the theater and do they remember you? Of course not. They remember that song as being by Bobby Darin. So I stood in the back of the theater and said to myself, "So this is where Bertolt Brecht worked. Wow." Okay, pilgrimage over; time to get back to West Berlin, where the Germans were at least happy.

We headed back to Paris and then home. The trip was an experience that has informed the way I look at things. There is a world out there, and people don't look at everything the way we do. For one thing, Europeans didn't divide their land into suburbs. They didn't have the cash, or, if they did, they weren't going to waste it that way. Besides, they seem to have better taste than we do.

That trip taught me that everyone should get out of the country and see other parts of the world. It's pretty sad that President Bush the Junior never had the intellectual curiosity to go abroad until he was in office. I still wonder how you can elect a leader of the free world who has never seen the world. For God's sake, the man never even made it to Canada. That's almost impossible. Even drunk on a bet you can make it to Canada.

If you don't go and see the rest of the world, you don't realize that they have something America does not—and that is culture. We don't have that. We are too young a nation to have a culture. The closest we come is when we leave yogurt in the fridge too long.

POT

Gateway to heroin

Lenny Bruce probably said it best—we are a nation of folks who like to get high. We are also a nation in which alcohol is legal and pot is not, even though there are millions who smoke the stuff in this country from all walks of life. And regimenting the means of escape that people use, as any asshole should know at this point, is a complete waste of time.

I had been a drinker in high school, as were all of my friends, but things took a turn when we all went off to college and discovered the wonders of cannabis. I have a feeling we smoked pot as much for the high as for the fact that it was taboo. Nothing makes for more fun than a good taboo, and pot was certainly a good taboo.

A friend of ours was in Vietnam and sent my friend Rick a joint. That's right, one joint that was then smoked by ten of us. And if you wonder why we lost that war—besides the fact that these folks had something to fight for besides Communism, like control of their own country and destiny—it may have been the pot.

Now, I had smoked pot a few times and enjoyed its titillations. It was like bubble gum for the brain. And while I still can't remember the first time I smoked up, I sure remember that joint we all shared at my friend Lenny's.

There haven't been many nights like that in my life. We sat in a huge circle, as behooves a ritual, and passed the joint around. I can't remember any of us having more than a puff and a half, and within just a few minutes we had liftoff. This was followed by a couple of booster rockets that sent us all into a space and time continuum that none of us had ever experienced.

I remember two major moments from that night: I laughed at the grass, and by doing so—don't ask me how, it's a drug for crying out loud—I felt at one with the universe. I had never felt this before. Delusional or not, it was something I never found at temple and it has been a comfort to me ever since. I don't know if feeling at one with the universe is real or not, but then, what difference does it make?

The euphoria was soon replaced with panic as the drug refused to wear off. I found myself in the bathroom pissing out what was left of it. And as I stared at the bubbles I was making in the bowl, they slowly transformed into the head of Abraham Lincoln as he appears on the penny. This Vietnamese pot had transported me to an even stranger land than Southeast Asia seemed to us at the time. For the life of me, I don't know how someone could smoke this shit in the jungle of a foreign country. We were having enough trouble coping with it in the familiar surroundings of Lenny's folks' house in the woods.

One of the girls completely freaked out, having never experienced anything like this before. (She was a good Catholic girl, and even the mass in Latin doesn't really get your head into shape for this type of experience.) We watched her in full panic mode, climbing onto the bed and screaming at us to stay away from her, although none of us were near her. She finally calmed down a little and spent the rest of the evening hiding under the bed. I know how she felt. I did exactly the same thing during the Reagan administration.

The rest of us spent most of the time laughing our teats off. There was one moment that I think will help you understand what I have been fumbling to try to explain. A Dylan album was playing on the stereo, and a group of us were sitting around, taking in all of the profundity we could possibly get from him. The song finished and we all started to chat about our lives—wishes, hopes, dreams, and what have you. There were five of us and we all had something to say. Then we all paused to try and figure out what the next song would be.

We thought we had been speaking for quite a while, when in fact we had the entire conversation in the time it takes an album to go from one song to the next. We had fallen into a bottomless well of time in the moment between two songs. Now, that, my friends, is what I call pot.

THE UNIVERSITY OF NORTH CAROLINA

Duke SUCKS!

Come sophomore year at the University of North Carolina, I had decided I would major in drama. But my plan was to take as many courses in other departments as possible in order to find a real major, one that might lead to a real job in the real world. I took psychology, but it involved too many rats and pigeons, plus statistics was a requirement, so the hell with that. I took sociology and a course called, get this, "The Negro," and I thought any department that had a course called "The Negro" was not a department with a subject I wanted to major in. I had to take some math courses, and I was good at math, but I didn't know what it was good for. I loved English—reading was the next best thing to music—but an English major was about as real as a drama major. I took education courses, but if I was going to teach theater, then I may as well just take drama.

Three weeks after I arrived at school, the head of the drama department dropped dead. That certainly didn't bode well for the future of my higher education, and it left the department in a bit of a shambles. They picked a temporary head of the department from the faculty and he referred to himself as the temporary head. As a result, as much as he would like to make decisions on a variety of issues, he couldn't . . . because he was only temporary. He was temporary for the entire time I was there.

I thought—and you are going to love this—that I wanted to be a drama critic. I know, I know. How fucked up is that? I thought it was like being a sportswriter, only it would be a mental game I'd be watching. I saw theater as a sporting event of the mind, and the actors were like athletes who either performed well or blew it. I also thought that there were a few really great drama critics but that the rest of them were total pricks who didn't understand that criticism was about helping not hurting. I guess I thought I would be the Albert Schweitzer of drama critics.

But one doesn't go to undergraduate drama school and major in criticism, so I had to find a different area in which to specialize. Well, acting was out. In case I still had any delusions that I might have talent as an actor, there were some terrific actors there who served as a reminder that I was not even in their ballpark. Hell, I wasn't even in the parking lot outside their ballpark.

I wasn't going to direct, because that meant you really had to know about acting. Technical theater was out because, well, I am not technical, so that left playwriting. I figured it wasn't fair for a critic not to have worked in the theater at least in some capacity, so I chose that as my specialty. And since I couldn't find anything else that I cared as much about in the giant book of courses, I entered the world of the theater.

I also joined a fraternity. That's not a typo, I really did. One of the things about UNC that I didn't realize when I applied was that there were seven guys to every girl. And let's face it, those odds were not going to work much in my favor. The University of North Carolina at Greensboro, the all-women's campus, had five thousand women, and the only way I had a shot at meeting them was by joining a fraternity. I figured if I could get them in a confined space I might have a chance.

I joined a nonsectarian fraternity called Pi Lambda Phi and met a terrific group of guys who were totally diverse. Half the house drank and the other half did drugs, and they would watch each other. It was highly entertaining. There were New York Jews and Southern Crackers, and being in the fraternity helped me get my bearings in the brave new world of the South. And believe me, I needed the help since it was also the only time I have ever heard anyone hurling anti-Semitic invectives my way.

On more than a few occasions, late on weekend evenings, the guys in a rival frat would stand on their porch and scream at us that we were kikes (even though there were far fewer Jews in the fraternity than Christians). I'll never forget standing there one night with Jim and Jack, both Christians, as these idiots spewed their nonsense. My friends wanted to kick their asses, but I talked them out of it. I have never seen a reason to waste energy on idiots.

I just couldn't get over the fact that that kind of shit still existed. In truth, I found very little of that kind of idiotic behavior down South. Though I do remember being amazed when a blind date said to me, "You're Jewish? I've never met a Jewish fellah before." Well, it certainly proved to be a red-letter day for her. Her first real live Jew. Unfortunately she didn't get to know me as well as I would have liked, and she missed out on the opportunity to see this Jew naked.

But for all the prejudice I encountered at school, an extraordinary teacher and mentor by the name of William Geer countered it. He taught a required course called Modern Civilization, and his wisdom was as abundant as his love of life. PBS chose him as one of the great American college professors and filmed a show about him that year.

He devoted much of his teaching to clearing our young minds of whatever type of prejudice we harbored, and anything else that limited our thinking. He loved to torture his Southern students by comparing the Reverend Billy Graham to Johann Tetzel, one of the chief sellers of the Catholic Church's indulgences. Just being around Professor Geer put my mind on the alert, and he never hesitated to support my endeavors and my outlook on life. I count myself extraordinarily lucky to have met a man like that. He provided an antidote to all the authority figures for whom I had no respect.

My roommate at the time was a beefy New Yorker from Pelham, named Leon Padula. We lived in a quad of rooms with two devout Christians—a North Carolina boy, who owned the most shoes I had ever seen, and a football player, who had quit the team. Shortly thereafter he quit school to join the army and went to Vietnam. I returned after Thanksgiving vacation and was met by one of the religious counselors assigned to my dormitory. He told me that Leon was dead. I told him he was crazy. I had just seen him five days earlier; it could not be true. Except that there are cars and accidents, and he had died in one. I learned three lessons from that horrifically sad event: First, there is only today; tomorrow is an afterthought. Second, your dream is what really counts, so always pursue it with a vengeance. And third, God can be a real prick sometimes.

Chapel Hill was an extraordinary place to go to school at that time. The South was still in the throes of the end of segregation and experiencing a huge upheaval. The university was referred to as a liberal bastion, but it was being compared to the rest of the state of North Carolina, there were still signs up like HOME OF THE NORTH CAROLINA KKK. The university wasn't paying a decent living wage to the mostly black cafeteria servers, so they went on strike and won. It was the first of many strikes I would see in my time at Chapel Hill, and the first voice of defiance outside of my own head.

C.S.A.

THE SIXTIES

***"There's something happening here/
What it is ain't exactly clear."***
—Buffalo Springfield

This is a good time to point out that it was the sixties when I went off to college. Never has a period in time, outside of the Dark Ages and the Spanish Inquisition, been so maligned. Many of my generation would go as far to say that it really never happened, that those of us who wax nostalgic about the period are just glamorizing a series of nonevents. Sorry, these idiots are full of shit. And I could list a few of them whom I know well, but I am too courteous to expose them. They missed the point. And they are the ones who made it seem worse than it was. One whom I met along the way put LSD into the oranges of kids taking buses from Yale to D.C., which was as perverted as his ultraconservatism is now.

The sixties did happen. And maybe our only cultural contribution was to tie-dye the world, but it was a hell of a time to be alive. And if you were paying attention, the lessons you could learn would serve you in good stead. It is certainly the period in which I completely went off the normal rails of socialization, never to really return.

The seeds of this period started for me when I was just twelve and watching a documentary hosted by Edward R. Murrow, called *Harvest of Shame*. It was an unflinching look at how migrant workers in America lived, and it completely floored me. All of the insulation the suburbs had given me now seemed like a sham. How could I be living like *this* when those who gathered our food were living like *that*?

Our lifestyle was built on the backs of the hard labor of a class kept in the chains of poverty with little or no conceivable way out. Kids my age were picking fruit. What in the name of fuck was going on here? As I write this, the changes in the system have been so minimal as to be absolutely stupefying. How could my family have so much when these families were lucky just to have clean running water?

But that wasn't the only disturbing footage I saw at the time. The television screen would also be filled with black-and-white images of violence, while peaceful black men and women began to integrate themselves into a white society. I had already begun to look at authority with a rather skeptical eye and it was only getting worse.

It's true that the sixties didn't work, but how could it have? Most of us were just kids with few real leaders, and the adult population, except for a scant few, was of absolutely no help. They wanted us to stay on track, keep our noses to the grindstone, and wait for them to tell us if there was anything we really needed to worry about. While we waited for our guidance, we got stoned. A lot.

Things really started to heat up over the Vietnam War. Isn't that always the way with wars—they are just so messy. Maybe we should try to avoid them. Especially if they aren't necessary, and, boy, was this a war that was unnecessary. The big brains behind President Kennedy had an idea called the domino theory. They figured if South Vietnam became Communist, it was just a matter of time before all of Southeast Asia became Communist. Who would have thought that a children's game could be the basis of a political theory? Of course, the fact that it was a game for kids is probably why it turned out to make no sense.

I only bring this up because the theory for the current war in Iraq is that once Iraq becomes democratic, everyone in the Middle East will immediately leap on the bandwagon. It's the original domino theory in reverse. Wow, it didn't work one way, so why not try it the other way? Besides, those Middle Easterners have always taken quite a shine to our way of life. They took a vote—they think it's less filling *and* tastes great.

Anyway, back to my flashback. . . . What made the Vietnam War a little sticky was the fact that there was a draft. A lot of young men were affected, and they were mostly the sons of a lot of guys who fought in World War II. But while that war was as easy to grasp as a Ping-Pong paddle, this war was a bit more difficult to understand, to say the least.

A whole bunch of kids in college, who had nothing but time on their hands to do a lot of research, were discovering a lot of stuff about the war in Vietnam that made no sense to them. It didn't seem like the kind of war for which you wanted to give up the ghost. When the first troops came home, they weren't all so gung ho for the whole thing either.

And television didn't help the government's case. Cameras followed these young kids through the jungles, and it just looked like we were completely out of our depth—except for the field commanders and the men in suits, who told us that it was just going swell, as the number of dead rose. I just stopped listening. I was sick of the death. Who were these leaders, where did they come from, and why didn't they seem to have a brain in their heads? They were supposed to know better, and if they didn't, then we sure did.

Then, of course, there were the drugs, which really don't help when it comes to taking this period of time seriously. Why everyone is so shocked that the youth of America does drugs is beyond me. *Every* generation of young Americans has done drugs. We were lucky, or maybe unlucky, depending on one's perspective, to have fallen into a time of hallucinogens. LSD, mescaline, psilocybin, and mushrooms made their way across the country. We took trips, aptly named, because we truly traveled; only, the trip was in our minds.

I actually took mescaline for my GREs. Responsible on my part, no; but boy was it fun. I mean, if you have to take a test and don't want to, it sure makes it interesting. I was the exam, the exam was me, and we were all together. Ironically I did better than when I was stone-cold sober for my SATs. This is not to suggest that it is a good idea, mind you. I *do not* advise trying this at home, kids. Besides, good mescaline is hard to come by nowadays, and the fact of the matter is, everyone can always get lucky.

On the flip side, my first trip on LSD was horrific, to say the least. I was with my friends Charley, Cliff, and Cliff's girlfriend, DeeDee, and we all took it. We took a ride, and I forget who was driving, but we drove into my old neighborhood, where I had lived from my birth to the age of seven. Here's a big tip: If you are going to take LSD, don't go back to your old neighborhood. It's not the place you want to be. You have way too many memories pounding the inside of your skull.

You see, LSD opens your brain to all sorts of images, many of which don't exist. It also informs your thought process in a way that is no longer linear, but more like a four-lane Mobius strip in a variety of changing colors with track lighting. I thought we were in at least four auto accidents before we got there. I remember being the only one who seemed to notice. Everyone seemed much more relaxed than I was, and I found it impossible to explain what was happening to me.

As I was losing contact with reality, the last thing I wanted to do was freak my friends out. They would have started worrying about me and their trips would have been ruined. Not only that, but their concern for me would have brought guilt into the equation—and guilt is enough on its own without the influence of LSD.

As it was, things got worse. When we stopped by some train tracks near my childhood home, I heard a train coming. I looked down the tracks and saw it. My friends were oblivious. As we stood away from the tracks, the train passed—and it was loaded with Nazi soldiers. I guessed they were headed to D.C. to discuss how the Vietnamese problem should be handled.

Of course, I was the only one who saw this train, as my friends were off discussing how the universe showed its love. It was only in my mind. My sanity moved a little closer to the edge of the abyss.

I was brought back when we stopped at McDonald's. "I'll do the ordering," Charley said. How he could talk to strangers and form words and be so eloquent completely baffled me.

Charley put in his order: "I'd like nine milkshakes, three vanilla, three strawberry, and three chocolate." When we got to the car and Cliff asked him why so many milkshakes, Charley said, "You never know when you might need another milkshake." And then he couldn't stop laughing. That eased my anxiety, but not by much. I still couldn't form words.

This experience was so different from the one I would witness later when my brother Ronnie flew down to North Carolina for Jubilee, a three-day music festival at Chapel Hill. The Allman Brothers were the centerpiece of the festivities and, trust me, we got very, very festive.

Now, Ronnie had done all sorts of drugs at this point, and he decided he wanted to celebrate the end of his school year with his first hit of acid. I decided to skip it so I could keep an eye on him. Jubilee was as good a place as any to do it because many of the folks who surrounded us were proficient in all ways psychedelic. We were fifteen rows from the stage, so it couldn't have been more perfect.

I knew the drug had begun to affect him when he asked me if this was an airplane landing strip and should he be worried about that. There were lots of lights that stretched the length of the field, and if one were a bit high, one might conceive that it was a landing strip—but then one would have forgotten that a concert was about to take place. I told him no. He asked if I was sure. I told him that I was positive. He looked around, took in the scene, and then laughed himself silly.

The band hit the stage and we could feel the entire audience lift off. It may not have been an airstrip, but this crowd was launched. I was just smoking pot, on top of a touch of speed, and a bit of Boone's Farm to take the edge off. (After all, as his older brother I had to be the responsible one. My parents would have been so proud.)

I actually found myself getting a contact high from all the folks tripping around me. I have never experienced that before or since. It was wild, to say the least, and I found it to be much easier on the neurons.

A few moments later my brother turned to me and said that he was about to lose verbal contact and that I should keep an eye on him. If he wasn't smiling, I should tap him on the shoulder, but he thought everything was going to be just fine. And it was.

No one I ever saw tripping on acid for the first time had the kind of understanding of the drug that my brother did. It takes a hell of a mind to be able to deal with that kind of drug. I was in awe.

It should be noted I am also a big fan of people like Martin Luther King Jr. and Mahatma Gandhi. They were great thinkers and remarkable men, I just don't know if they ever took acid. Either way, when it came to taking acid, Ronnie was definitely in their league. Rule to live by: It's important to put everything into perspective.

I wish I had known that on my first LSD trip. By the time we returned to the apartment where we had started our adventure, I had forgotten my name. *Warning! Warning! Warning! This might be one of the reasons you may not want to take LSD! Forgetting your name provokes anxiety! Anxiety is not fun!*

I tried stumbling through the alphabet for clues, but that was of no help. Then I picked up a dictionary to see if there were any words that might help remind me of my given name, the one I had spent every day of my life with.

I finally realized I could look in my wallet. Yes, yes, yes, there would be all sorts of things with my name on it in my wallet. Oh wait, no, no, no, what if I open it up and there is nothing but Monopoly cards in there? I couldn't stop laughing. At that point I didn't have to look in my wallet. I remembered my name. The rest of the evening was much more enjoyable, as I floated around on a marshmallow floor, as we discussed the finer points of how grand existence was.

You call an evening like that fun? Is that your idea of a good time? This is what the sixties were all about. And, if nothing else, the decade tried to teach me to relax about whatever was coming my way. Obviously it is not a lesson that I learned all that well.

In 1964 there was a picture of a be-in in San Francisco on the cover of *Life* magazine. It was a foldout photo with hundreds of thousands of people crowded into Golden Gate Park, all decked out in tie-dyes and bell-bottoms. It signaled that a new age was coming. Things were going to be different, as were we. Years later I read in a book by Emmet Grogan, a prominent figure in the San Francisco hippie scene, that this had all been staged by the fashion designers of the city to sell their wares to the world. It wasn't even real. It was an advertisement.

The sixties were over before they really ever even started. And rightfully so. From the beginning, the sixties were a matter of style over content. That seemed to be the major lesson that we left the world. If you've got style, you don't need content. He who creates the nicest packaging, could, dare I say, rule the world.

THE UNIVERSITY OF NORTH CAROLINA AGAIN

"Living La Vida Loca"

By my junior year, war protests on campus had started to move into full swing. And these weren't the only kind of protests being staged. Black students had seriously begun to question their educations at predominantly white universities, and ghettos in major cities were torched out of frustration with an economic system that left little mobility for those in poverty. This, of course, was seen by many as the end of the known universe.

There was definitely a schism, and it wasn't just between those who were for the war and those who were against it. It was between those who felt there was a way things always *had* been done and those who believed there was a way things *could* be done. Both sides were wrong. Both sides were angry. Both sides were arrogant.

But God, they were breathless, exciting times. I imagine this was the way Hemingway must have felt when he ran with the bulls. Things were changing. My first year at school there was a parade down the main street of town, led by a fraternity guy dressed in a Confederate uniform. This was in 1967. The Confederacy had lost the war just over a hundred years before, but tradition dies hard in the

South. By the following year, that nonsense was dead and buried. No one was going to wear a Confederate uniform on that campus unless it was Halloween and he wasn't going out that night.

As had happened at many other campuses throughout the country, the black students took over the administration building at Duke University to protest the lack of a black studies program. Many of the white students sympathized and gathered in solidarity, hoping to keep the police from taking the students out of the building until their demands were met. This was at a time when segregation was still pretty much the norm in Durham, North Carolina. Jesse Helms—yes, the one who later became senator—owned a television station and came on one night with a gun in his hand and told his viewers that they, too, needed to arm themselves in order to protect their rights.

Like I was saying, the fun never stopped.

So I went on over to Duke to see my friends Ray and Tom and to find out what was going on. Within a few hours, as darkness fell, the cops made their move, and for the first time I smelled tear gas and felt the power of authority when it doesn't understand what it is up against. I awoke the next morning a different person, as the tear gas still hung in the air over the Duke campus.

During the summer of 1968 the fateful and riot-fueled Democratic National Convention was held in Chicago. I really wanted to go. I walked out the door of my house, suitcase in hand, prepared to sneak off and do my part to change my country's destiny. Once again my mother stopped me.

"Where do you think you're going?"

"Chicago, " I replied.

"You want to get killed? We can kill you right here at home. It'll save you a trip."

So I watched the riots unfold on television in my family's den. That November, Richard Nixon was elected president and nausea ruled the land. Part of me still blames my mother for that.

I wrote my first play during my junior year, and it was worse than awful. I was taking my first class in playwriting and we were supposed to finish a one-act play by the end of the semester. My professor was a well-respected academic who had written texts both on playwriting and technical theater. He was extremely old but very sharp.

As the semester drew to a close we would read our plays aloud in class. What was wondrous and startling about this exercise was that our professor would always fall asleep while we were reading. You wouldn't be more than a few pages in when he would nod off. And just before you read the last few pages, he would wake up.

He did this with everyone, whether it was a good play or not. Then he would give an absolutely insightful interpretation of the work and how to improve it. It was like a magic trick. None of the students ever asked about this habit of his; we just stood in amazement. It wasn't until years later, when I understood the process, that I realized everyone makes pretty much the same mistakes in their first work. And since we had made those very mistakes, he seemed like a genius to us. The guy was always on target.

Play in hand, I went to meet with the temporary head of the drama department to see whether he minded if I got a couple of actors to present it in one of the classrooms in the building. He said he couldn't really approve it since he was only the temporary head of the drama department. He explained—again—that if he were the real head of the department, he would approve it, but his hands were tied.

I was prepared for this type of double talk; I had read *Catch 22,* and my professor sounded exactly like Major Major Major Major. He said that I could do it without approval but that I would have to deal with any consequences that might arise. And since it didn't seem like anyone could possibly take issue with it, I went ahead and produced, on my own, my very first play.

It made me sick. I would tell you what it was about, but it would make you sick too. I stood at the back of the room, facing the wall. Each line of dialogue was like a knife in my back. I spent the whole play quivering as if I had malaria. It's amazing that I ever wrote another. It was not fun.

At the end of my junior year I was approached by a couple of representatives from the student senate to run for office for my off-campus district. For the life of me, I don't remember how they knew me, but I will never forget why they asked me to run. My name would be the first one on the ballot and, therefore, if history ran true to form, I would win. It worked—I won. You've got to love democracy in action.

I guess I ran because I still had this notion that somehow my presence in the system would make a difference. With a volatile student body, upset by the war and freaked out by the draft, it seemed like an exhilarating time to be involved in student government. Also, students were gaining a larger voice in the way the university was evolving, and that seemed exciting. God, if only this were true.

Representative government may be exciting in that British parliamentary way where everybody is always yelling or crying out something like "Hazzah, hazzah," but although the senate of the University of North Carolina was somewhat interesting, it certainly was not exciting. It was a series of routine movements of student funds and activities. But with campuses everywhere poised to strike over the war, there was the occasional debate that added some much-needed drama to the proceedings.

The first strike, in October, culminated in a march on Washington. Campuses around the country were brought to a halt as students stopped attending classes. Certainly not a difficult thing for the student body to do.

On the day of the strike, one of the more irritating members of our illustrious student government decided that since he found this activity reprehensible, he would punish those on his committee who were striking. He called three meetings, and when the striking members didn't show up, they were, by virtue of the constitution, thrown off the committee and replaced by others who thought the war was just a lovely notion and anyone who was against it was a raging Communist pinko maggot slut.

Well, this truly pissed off the liberal wing. They felt that it was such an abuse of power that the committee chairman should be impeached. His actions certainly angered me to no end. At the very least I thought we should yell at him for a couple of hours—just to make sure he understood how big an asshole he was.

The liberals approached me and asked if I would be the one to raise the articles of impeachment. I agreed under the condition that I didn't have to be the one to conduct the legal proceedings that would follow. No problem, I was told, there would be others who would handle that. Perfect, let's get the prick, I said.

Yeah, let's get the prick. Well, it would have been nice if any of us had read the constitution. I should have known that these guys were as lazy as I was. And if they were really that lazy, then why weren't they glad to be thrown off the committee? So now I was stuck as the lawyer for the impeachment process. I have never had any interest in the law. That and medicine left me cold, and I am just thrilled that there are people who want to do that shit.

I couldn't really get myself to focus on the task at hand, and I certainly didn't know how to express myself in my role as prosecutor. Meanwhile, my worthy opponent was in law school and knew his shit. It did nothing but frustrate and irritate me, so after an inept attempt at actually trying to work within the system, I was pissed off at both sides. I was embarrassed by my own incompetence and didn't have enough orifices for all the ways these idiots were screwing me. At that point I'd had enough. I told them that I wasn't going to be a whipping boy for their stupidity and walked out of the chambers, never to seek another elected office, anywhere, again.

I also wrote my first full-length play during that year—a musical, no less. I didn't write the music; it was written by my friend Cary Engelberg. He was attending George Washington University and they were opening a new theater there. We called the musical *Do You Know Where Your Children Are?* The title was based on a familiar refrain played constantly on television: "It's eleven o'clock, do you know where your children are?" It was about our lives growing up in the suburbs, with a lot of artistic license and embellishments. The set was a model of a DNA helix, which seemed very profound at the time.

Cary wrote some great music and we had a few laughs here and there, but the play ran two and a half hours without an intermission. Instinctively I think we knew that if we gave the audience a chance to leave they would run like hell. Which is exactly what Cary did. While I had definitely been bitten by the theater bug (which would prove to be a perfect profession for an obsessive-compulsive personality like mine), he turned his back on the theater and is now a doctor of note at the University of Michigan, where he specializes in infectious diseases.

What a waste. In a world desperately in need of bad theater, I'll never understand why Cary is throwing his life away helping sick people. Hey, some people have to learn from their own mistakes.

THE FINAL STRIKE

Four dead in Ohio

Toward the end of the school year Nixon began bombing Cambodia, which did not sit well with America's already angry students. Enough was enough. Campuses erupted with protests. At Kent State, as we all now know too well, there was a protest that ended in the death of four students at the hands of National Guardsmen. What they were doing with live ammunition is beyond me.

Many conspiracy theorists opined that the killing of these students was a strategy of the government to keep us in line, that somehow we had it coming to us. I doubt it. The government is never that smart, and thinking isn't their strong suit.

At the time, many of us felt that Nixon and the creeps with whom he had surrounded himself were thrilled about what had happened. It was the last straw. With just a few weeks to go until exams, campus after campus went on strike. There were those in school who supported the war, and they no doubt felt that we were striking so we wouldn't have to take exams. I consider that a lot of bullshit. Although, as a senior it was nice not to have to worry about those last few days of tests.

Besides, there were other things on my mind. It was spring, a time of rebirth and wonder. I was in the very heart of my youth. And my country was bombing the snot out of a tiny little country in Southeast Asia, and there but for the grace of God, I could have been lying in a pool of blood. It made me want to do something. As dumb as shutting down a college is, it was at least something. It was the only tool we had and we used it.

I wanted to help. So I approached a few members of the strike mobilization committee to find out how I could take a more active part in what was going on. Since there wasn't much I could do at my campus, I came up with a brilliant idea. I got permission to go over and help organize the women's campus at Greensboro since they had not, as of yet, joined in the strike.

I know what you're thinking. And you're right. Volunteering served a dual purpose. I could help the young women at UNCG see the error of their ways, and I could also help them err in their ways. Rarely is one presented with the opportunity to satisfy both one's moral and immoral convictions simultaneously.

Let it be known, I wasn't successful on either count. The girls never went on strike and I struck out. Maybe if I had done my job properly, the Age of Aquarius would still be upon us.

JUBILEE

"Rock and roll never forgets."
—Bob Seger

One thing is for sure—at UNC we really knew how to party. The three-day music festival, Jubilee, was the final campus blowout of the year; the event was so spectacular, it should have been called Jubifuckinleeeee. It was of epic proportions, with the best entertainment imaginable. During my time there they managed to gather some of the best musical acts playing at the time, all of the bands at the peak of their popularity—acts like Blood Sweat & Tears and the Allman Brothers. In my senior year alone we had Joe Cocker's Mad Dogs and Englishmen, James Taylor, B. B. King, and Grand Funk Railroad.

James Taylor's first album had just been released that spring. He was from Chapel Hill and his dad headed up the medical school. And when he sang "Carolina in My Mind," we all went nuts, screaming at each other as our fevered, pot-addled minds hoped to grasp the entire depth of what this song meant. In the end it meant nothing, but it was pretty fucking awesome at the time. And when you are in Carolina listening to James, you actually see the "Fire and Rain."

Then there was Grand Funk Railroad, a group that had a very limited shelf life. They didn't survive the sixties. As they say, I guess you had to be there. They managed to nail down the simplest chords and driving drums to keep any stoned soul delighted and amused. Maybe it was the joy of monotony, but at the time there was no one like them. The true star of the weekend was Joe Cocker and his Mad Dogs and Englishmen tour, featuring a cast of soon to be all-star performers. Rita Coolidge, Leon Russell, the Shelter Horns, to name but a few.

My friends Ed and Cliff had come down for the weekend, and Tom and Ray had come over from Duke. Ray's girlfriend, Geri, had gotten some of her sorority sisters from Duke to come as our friends' dates. And we all gathered at the place I was sharing with Don, who had transferred from the University of Maryland. I had the bright idea to bake up some pot brownies, having never experimented with the herb in that fashion. Only there was one problem, no brownie mix—I guess there had been a rush on it that weekend. There wasn't even any chocolate pudding. Hell-bent on experimenting, I bought vanilla pudding.

I soon discovered that there are a couple of problems with using vanilla. First, it does an awful job of masking the flavor of grass and makes for a truly lousy presentation. Compound this with the fact that I didn't remove the stems and seeds from the pot and, well . . . voilà, a bowl of baby puke. If Martha Stewart had been around at the time, she would have had an aneurysm.

I can still remember the sour looks on the sorority girls' faces as we left to go to the concert. Ray and I got into his car with Geri and my girlfriend at the time, Cindy Champion. (How great a name is that?) They weren't really upset because they were used to this kind of nonsense from us. We backed the car up and pulled out of the parking lot. Ray and I chattered away about how bad my experiment tasted but that it felt pretty nice. And I apologized up and down to Geri for screwing things up for her friends.

We'd been driving for a while when Geri leaned over to Ray and pointed out that we weren't moving. She thought the back wheels were in a ditch or something. Ray and I looked out the window, looked back at each other, and then looked back out the window. Then we both had one of those laughs that goes on for so long that it ends with tears—tears of stupid joy, mind you, not of judgmental recrimination. We both thought we were moving. So much for the concept of pot and safe driving.

It made for a hell of a concert, though, I can tell you that. At least, I'm pretty sure I can . . .

JOHN-JOHN THE DOG

Who knew that when the avatar showed up it would be a cocker-terrier mix.

My senior year at Chapel Hill I made the decision that if I wasn't going to have a relationship I was going to have a dog. My parents never let us have one because my father was afraid of them. So we had parakeets, which are nice if you want to teach your children about death. Our first parakeet was old when we got him, so not only was he senile, he was also very mean. The others lasted a few months until they either flew into a mirror or ate the plastic toys that littered the bottom of the tray—a kind of parakeet suicide, I believe.

I had always wanted a dog and it seemed like the perfect time to get one. Who knows, I thought, the dog might even lead me into a relationship. "He's not that cute, but he's got a cute dog, and one out of two ain't bad."

A friend of mine mentioned that there was a woman in Greensboro, North Carolina, who had a kennel. It was packed with more than sixty dogs and they were all named after the Kennedys. Her husband had given her an ultimatum and she had to start giving the dogs away. There was Teddy and Robert and Jackie and Caroline and Rose, to name but a few, and I got a six-month-old cocker-terrier named John-John.

The first thing I tried to do was change his name. I didn't want to be standing around the middle of campus yelling, "John-John, John-John!" I wanted a tougher name for a little dog like that. But he wasn't having it. That's the name he responded to, and that's the way he wanted it.

This was a dog of inordinate intelligence, and he didn't have time for my bullshit. He was the sort of dog that looked in your eyes with a kind of wistfulness, as if to say, "Gee, it's sad you're not as evolved as I am." And I probably wasn't, as I was just a college kid.

It took him a couple of days to be house trained, and shortly after that he didn't even need a leash. There were no leash laws in Chapel Hill at the time (wonder what the PETA people think about that), and he liked to walk right next to me. A few weeks later we were walking home and he darted into the middle of the street. A car ran right over him and luckily did not hit him, but it obviously scared the ever-loving shit out of him. He never left the sidewalk again and would always stand at a corner and wait for the light before he'd cross the street. He socialized himself faster than I did when I was a child.

John-John would go to class with me, and when the professor got boring he would split and wait outside for me. As he got to know my friends, he would follow them around while I was in class. Or he'd go and wait for me at one of their houses. If I was in a restaurant and he saw friends of mine walk by, he'd run outside and walk them to the corner and then come back to the restaurant. Within just a few months he always knew how to find me or knew where to go so that I could find him.

I went to Duke with him one night to see a girl there. I left him outside the dormitory, and when I came out a

few hours later he was gone. I waited but he never showed up. I searched but couldn't find him. The next evening, he showed up at the dorm at exactly the same time I had brought him there the night before.

He was an amazing animal who never ceased to astound me. It was as if *he* had trained *me*. I was lucky to have an animal like that as my owner.

TECHNOLOGY MY ASS

Staring into the void

It is precisely at this point in writing the book that my laptop broke down on me in a hotel room in Madison, Wisconsin. It didn't just break down. It dropped dead.

The amazing thing about computers is that they are magical, especially if you don't know shit about how they work. They're really wonderful pieces of equipment, and when they don't work, you realize just how much you need them and just how unnecessary they truly are. I would have actually written this book with a pencil if I didn't have something called a "deadline." Maybe that's why the computer broke down, just to say to me, "Why don't you take that pencil and shove it up your ass. Yeah, I may be unnecessary, but you desperately need me."

So my computer is now lying dead in front of me. The computer is less than a year old. So I guess this would be considered crib death.

Now, if they are going to make these machines so that they die within a year and it's supposed to be a disposable kind of thing, then they should just tell us. Don't put a warranty on it. Just tell us that in eleven months, we need to buy a new computer and transfer the files from the old one before it implodes and becomes about as useful in the writing process as an eggplant.

So I did what every computer illiterate does when staring at a dead computer that has a three-year warranty on it. I called tech support. Tech support is actually code for "No one is here, no one has ever been here. We could give a shit. You didn't pay enough for this thing in the first place, and besides, it works by magic." What they actually said on the other end of the phone was that they could give me precisely two minutes of technical advice, and they felt that in those two minutes, they could tell me everything I needed to know about fixing my computer.

At that point, with the amount of rage building up at the fact that my computer had broken down just when I was finally getting something written with a deadline beating on my head, I looked at the phone and wanted to bash my forehead into the little buttons. *But no,* the better part of my brain cried out, *it won't bleed. There won't be any satisfaction in listening to the technician moaning that my two minutes weren't up yet. For God's sake, let's see what they can do, then go bash* their *brains out.*

As I put the receiver back to my ear, I hear them babbling on the other end that it's $2.99 for each additional minute. That's right. You heard correctly: $2.99 for each additional minute. Oh, those two dollar and ninety-nine cent minutes must be just splendid—minutes of hope, minutes of wonder, minutes of infinite pleasure. "C'mon, tell me I'm the best, tell me no one else has ever manipulated your keyboard like this, tell me what to input. . . . *C'mon, tell me, god damn it!*"

But by then, I didn't care. I would have paid anything just to see my screen pop into action again. They had me by the nuts. They could have said ten dollars a minute and I would have paid it.

Now I know how those guys feel late at night, horny to the point of hysteria, after pulling up one of those over-the-top, girls-in-heat-just-for-you Web sites, reaching for the phone to dial a "Who's your daddy" 800 number and talk to a real person who cares about their boners. I, too, was all hot and sweaty as I waited for the information that would put my life back on track.

And I waited and I waited and I waited. And then, just to break up the monotony, I waited some more until, finally, a human being *never* got back to me. It made for a rich, full day, let me tell you. I had to soak in a hot tub for more than an hour and then take a nap just to get things back in order. At $2.99 a minute, I should have hung up and called one of those hot chix numbers, just to take the edge off. I would have, too, if I hadn't maxed out my credit card on tech support.

CELL PHONES

"Can you hear me now?"
—Verizon advertising slogan

While we're on the subject of machines that can drive one to madness, let's talk about cellular phones. I don't want to dwell on it, because my heart can't take it. For starters, the rate structures are completely incomprehensible, much like Medicare reform, which is actually written in Latin.

No one knows what the rates mean until the first bill arrives. Hell, nobody knows what the rates mean even after the second or third or hundredth bill arrives. What the hell are "county wireless license taxes" and "federal wireless number pooling and portability charges" anyway? Fuck if I know!

Only in this day and age can we come up with a device that makes us feel that we are getting convenience when in fact it is nothing but inconvenient. When you desperately need your cell phone, there is no juice left. And those nights when you fear your car will break down on that lonely stretch of road, you thank God you have a cellular phone and can call for help. . . . But there won't be any service in the middle of Hoohah, USA. There never is. They don't build towers there. Folks are afraid they won't be able to birth any more babies with a big-ass tower pumping them full of God knows what. So you'll just be sitting at the side of the road, waiting for the guy with the hook to come and kill you.

And I guarantee you this. After he's knocked you to the ground and he's about to swing that big old meat hook at your head, his fucking phone will ring. Somehow, psychopaths always get service.

NEW HAVEN

Haven, my ass!

After graduation I made the decision with my friends Tom, Cliff, and Ed to spend the summer months in New Haven, Connecticut. All right, folks, here's a tip. I don't know much; I act like I do, but I don't really. One thing I do know is that whenever you have vacation time of any sort, one of the last places you should consider going is New Haven, Connecticut. Despite the fact that it's the home of Yale University, it is truly one of the uglier places on the face of the earth.

It has to be really, really sunny for it not to seem gray. But to its credit, the city does offer a good submarine sandwich and a rather nice burger, but you can get that stuff in much nicer places. The biggest problem with New Haven is that there is more gravity there. I have seen this in only one other city—Greensboro, North Carolina. The pull of gravity is such that you never really feel good—you always feel weighted down and depressed.

Yale University sat in the midst of an economically depressed neighborhood, which gave it the feel of living in feudal England. There was a small community of activists who had gathered in this part of town and had started up such things as a food co-op, an automobile shop, and a soup kitchen. The whole community wasn't making enough money to shop at the supermarket, so we went to the co-op, where for a buck you could get a delightful meal of brown rice, vegetables, and salad. Just the memory of it makes me want to go to the bathroom.

New Haven, at that time, was a focal point for radical activity because it was the home of the Bobby Seale trial. There was a small Black Panthers contingent living on the outskirts of Yale University, and they were extremely militant because they were tired of the black community being screwed. (Militant is actually kind of a shitty word for them.) These guys were not a very happy lot.

Bobby Seale was the minister of information for the party, and even the president of Yale, Kingman Brewster Jr., had said that he didn't think Seale would get a fair trial in New Haven—a statement that certainly riled up mainstream America. The Panthers' headquarters was located downtown, and it seemed the police would harass them on a weekly basis. So Cliff, Ed, Tom, and a number of other very white, very middle-class kids took action. To show our solidarity—and feed our collective paranoia—we would form a human barricade in front of their headquarters just in case the police arrived. And the Panthers would always come out and yell at us.

In retrospect, I can understand their reaction. It must have been really insulting to them that a bunch of long-haired, hippie white kids had appointed themselves protection for the toughest black militants this country had ever seen. They probably thought we were merely playing at revolution. We weren't—we were just doing what we could.

The reason we decided to spend the summer in New Haven was that my friend Ed had gone to Yale and met some people who were putting together a new endeavor. It was something so idealistic that we must have been completely out of our minds. Even as I write this, I'm shaking my head in disbelief—especially since we now live in a world where "liberal" is a dirty word. We actually wanted to write and publish a left-wing *Reader's Digest*.

What's that, Lewis, you ask?

A misdirection of optimism, that's for sure. The idea behind it was that if we could appeal with simple intelligence to the American people about the war, civil rights, and economic justice, we could change their minds. To put it another way, we were hoping to update the paintings of Norman Rockwell by expressing our beliefs in a nonconfrontational fashion. We would write about our common concerns and interview people who would appeal to middle America.

Yep, obviously we were nuttier than fruitcakes, but we were just putting our money where our mouths were. And even though I had a fellowship in playwriting in the offing, I was hoping my involvement in this venture would lead me out of theater, where I still wasn't sure I belonged. I was looking for one more shot at being a part of society, albeit at its fringes, and avoiding outpatient clinics.

We lived in the basement of an art supply storefront. There was no kitchen and we slept on mattresses on the floor. The reason we lived like that was because we were broke. But these kinds of conditions do give you the sense that you're doing something important, perhaps because they don't pay people to do really important things. Albert Schweitzer and Mother Theresa did not die rich. And we certainly weren't getting paid; we were doing all of this on spec.

My first and only job on the magazine was to interview General Shoup, who had served in Vietnam and later declared the war unwinnable. He felt that we were making a huge mistake and it had to stop. According to General Shoup, we were fighting a group of people who were trying to unite their country and were sick of being under the thumb of a foreign power. I spent three or four hours with this stately gentleman who had served his country for forty or more years, and he made it quite clear to me that the course we had taken in Vietnam was madness. He told the story in a way that all those reading our version of *Reader's Digest* could understand. Too bad it was never printed.

As the summer unfolded it became quite obvious that we were not going to be able to pull off this magazine. The man who was funding it left town to search for his guru, like so many others at that time. For many of my generation, the path to enlightenment started with drugs and ended with gurus. I didn't quite understand how one followed the other, but meditation was becoming the next big thing. It seems to work for millions of people, so who am I to argue? Still, I figure you can close your eyes and listen to your own breath, or you can close your eyes and touch yourself—either way, you're going to end up in the same blissful state.

POWDER RIDGE

"If I don't get some shelter, oh yeah, I'm going to fade away."
—Rolling Stones

When the magazine endeavor failed, it dawned on us that we weren't going to get paid. Even in the face of destitution, we felt that it was important to finish the project. My friends are good that way. Also, there was a big rock festival coming up in Powder Ridge that we didn't want to miss. It was that kind of priority that had kept us going through the summer. Between being broke and living on the edge of dysentery from a bad vegetarian diet, the concert was our light at the end of the tunnel.

We were absolutely ecstatic the night of the festival. We had armed ourselves with a balanced diet of LSD, marijuana, and Boone's Farm apple wine. For those of you who have never experienced the quality of nausea brought on by a bottle of Boone's Farm, suffice it to say, it was the wine cooler of the sixties.

Cocktails in tow, we made our way to Powder Ridge, a dopey little ski resort not far from New Haven. The crowd was huge, and it was grand; we hadn't really seen many people that summer. And there were women there! We hadn't been seeing them at all.

The main artist playing that evening was a group called Rhinoceros. The band was kind of like the low-rent Phish of its time or a Grateful Dead that didn't quite make the grade. It didn't matter to us; it could have been a bad bar mitzvah band for all we cared. We were just thrilled to be out and about.

Once we had settled in on the hillside, it was time to take the LSD. My first trip had been an obvious horror show and I wasn't going to let that happen again. I had brought John-John the dog with me, and I felt that since he was living at a higher level than I was, he would watch over me—and fend off any evil, bad vibrations, or juju that might be in the area. He would keep a safe circle around me. Chances are anyone who has thoughts as crazy as these before taking acid won't get any crazier.

We'd just taken our LSD when it was announced that they needed folks to come down and help out with the parking. And we would get armbands! After a summer of feeling completely disenfranchised, we were about to become "The Man"—or at least a very "special" adult safety patrol. And maybe we would even meet some ladies! And even if we didn't, we would still have the armbands.

Our assignment was simple. All we had to do was make sure cars entering the parking lot took a left. If they took a right, they would end up stuck on a hillside and they'd need tow trucks to get them out. That was it. That was all we had to do. So we stood out there for a while, armbands akimbo, informing all that passed by to turn left. The sun began to set slowly and it was becoming more beautiful every millisecond.

Now, beauty is always relative. On LSD a beautiful sunset is not only a beautiful sunset, it is the beginning and the end of time as we know it; it is emblematic of all that is wondrous in nature; it is all of the joyousness of humanity expressed in the sky; it is how we are all connected to everything and everything is connected to everything else; it simply becomes a symphony unto itself, and the colors stagger you and you can't find the words to express all that you are feeling.

Again, maybe you had to be there.

Anyway, we decided we needed to sit down in order to truly appreciate a sunset of that magnitude. We had to talk about the sunset and what it meant to us, and what a summer it had been, even though things had gone bad, and weren't these the best armbands ever. It was like . . . well . . . in the ads they call it Miller Time. But this was Miller Time in another dimension and in Technicolor—and without the smell of stale beer and urine hanging in the air.

We talked and talked and talked about our hopes and dreams and visions of the future. Our reverie was disturbed by a cacophony of voices yelling and screaming. Night was now upon us, and when we rose to see what the commotion was all about, we noticed that some cars had taken a right instead of a left and were now stuck on the hill. Oh shit, we'd forgotten all about our job. So we took off our armbands, threw them under the nearest car, and walked slowly back to the hillside. It was exactly what every responsible drug user would have done.

The rock concert began and it was absolutely wonderful. Well, anything would have been absolutely wonderful that night. Between the LSD and the complete lack of any stimulus other than politics for more than two months, we were riding in high gear. It was a night of pure and simple avoidance. We avoided thinking about the fact that we were now out of college and what the fuck we were going to do on the heels of our failed venture. So we partied like there was no tomorrow. It was Boone's Farm for everybody.

The band took a short break and I walked down the hill with John-John to check things out. I went over to the bummer tent, a true product of the sixties. The tent was set up for those people who took drugs and weren't having a very good time of it.

Now, most of the time you couldn't be too sure of the quality of the drug. Although, in my experience the stuff was always of a very high quality, because back then we didn't have business majors peddling lower-quality stuff in an effort to increase profits. In the sixties there was no such thing as a business major. Business majors began to blossom in the eighties, and there's something profoundly stupid about the whole concept. There are just too many kinds of businesses to possibly major in all of them. For instance, there's the business of selling chairs and there's the completely different business of making chairs. The only thing they have in common is the need for an accountant.

Well, back when I was in school, people didn't major in business. They majored in chemistry because chemistry was big back then. And what did they do with their chemistry degrees? They made drugs for the rest of us. As a result, there was a lot of quality control because the chemists who were making the drugs wanted to take them too. Besides, it would have been tough to give someone a bad drug, because they knew you and would then beat the crap out of you.

But even if the drug was good, it was impossible to tell

what someone's reaction to it would be, and so the bummer tent came into being. A person could go to the tent and talk to a doctor or to other folks who had taken drugs before and understood the culs-de-sac that people might find themselves in. So I went over to the tent as an observer because now that I was having such a good trip, I thought John-John and I could help these poor folks out. John-John was obviously a huge help to me at this point; maybe I could get him to share his expertise with others.

There wasn't too much action in the tent, but I sat down and listened to a conversation between a few Californians, who had helped organize the event, and a group of the more prominent leaders of our tiny New Haven community. They were arguing over whether a Black Panther should speak to the crowd. The New Haven group didn't think it was a very good idea, but the more progressive West Coasters enjoyed combining their drugs, rock and roll, and politics all in one big cauldron. I had no interest in mixing all that stuff up. It would be like mixing cheap tequila shots with elevator music and a Dr. Phil lecture.

As I listened to this conversation I thought, *Wow, these guys are only a couple of years older than me, and if these are the people in charge, we are completely and utterly fucked. No wonder we're not getting anywhere. There are no adults in the room!*

It was finally decided that the Black Panther should speak. This was going to be good. I headed back to find my friends to wait for the disaster to unfold.

By the time I found them, the Black Panther had begun to speak. As he yelled at us for doing drugs, you could hear thunder in the distance, and heat lightning began to flash across the sky. It was the kind of thing that you see in your head when you listen to "In the Hall of the Mountain King." This really didn't help his cause. Under the influence of drugs, the crowd sensed that the Black Panther was causing the storm. It had been so nice out when the rock and roll was playing, and now it felt like there was something malevolent in the air.

This really sent the kids into a tailspin, and the more he spoke the more kids started heading down the hill toward the bummer tent. John-John, I am happy to report, kept my circle of safety intact. As the speech drew to a conclusion he started to tell us that if we really cared about our community we should get a gun and use it against the pigs. He suggested we should start by going after whoever was in charge of parking.

To be honest, I'm not sure if the last part actually happened or if it was just in my head. What I am confident about is that it started to drizzle and the concert was ruined. It was yet another bad night in our desperate attempt to establish a new kind of American community.

We left New Haven shortly thereafter. It was a summer that I would always remember, but it was a summer that I never wanted to relive. We were a little older, a little wiser, and a little more disillusioned.

FEAST

Writing may just be an excuse to have the whole day to masturbate.

Just before I graduated, the drama department informed me that I was being given a fellowship in playwriting from the Shubert Foundation. I pretty much won it by default, as there weren't any other playwrights around. My play *Do You Know Where Your Children Are?* may have sucked, but it allowed me to postpone entering the real world for at least another year. I could stay in the theater and pursue the insane career of writing plays without having to return to the much overhyped reality.

At this point I basically knew how to type a play, but I had no real idea of what went into writing a play. I decided that I would try to put together a company of actors, made up of whoever was available from the drama department, plus a few others from around campus. My hope was that by working with them I might figure out what I was supposed to be doing.

I approached the temporary head of the drama department—the same beacon of ineffectualness who couldn't give me authorization to perform my first play—and asked if it would be possible for the department to sponsor a production that I would write for the actors in the program who weren't involved in the department's main production. Again, he said he couldn't really authorize it because his position was temporary. (To this day, I have never met anybody with more job security than this temporary guy. He had almost made it an art form.)

So I went to the student activities board and asked for a thousand dollars to produce my play. I said I wouldn't spend a dime until I was sure we had a play worth doing. I hadn't written a word yet, but they gave me the go-ahead.

With my friend Jeff Davis, who was the organizational mastermind since my skills in that capacity were minimal, we held auditions, gathered our actors, and selected a director, Roy Underhill, whom everyone seemed to like. We found a couple of people interested in doing music, and I had some friends, Charley Huntley, Bill Hatch, and H. B. Hough, in the film program who would do whatever filming might be necessary. It was a time when multimedia shows were very big, and I thought utilizing a few other artistic disciplines might help cover my mistakes.

Now I just had to come up with a play. The only idea I had was for a loose structure in which we would follow a suburban youth as he grew up, and I would make up television spots to reflect the times, which included a commercial for a feminine hygiene spray for him and her and another for a cologne for real men called Dawgbalz. I figured that by distilling the collective stories and experiences of the group to come up with the scenes, I could learn about playwriting from the actor's viewpoint, as I clearly hadn't learned the process from being a playwright.

Michael Bennett, I would like to point out, used much the same device a few years later when he gathered the collective stories and experiences of Broadway dancers for a groundbreaking little show called *A Chorus Line*. That 1975 offering, which coincidentally opened at Broadway's

Shubert Theater, would go on to win nine Tony Awards and the Pulitzer Prize for drama.

Now, don't get me wrong, I am not taking credit for inspiring *A Chorus Line,* but I do believe the operative words here are "collective stories and experiences" and "Shubert." And, yes, the same approach of gathering "stories and experiences" was used before—most notably for the Bible, but that was centuries earlier and the idea pretty much laid fallow until, well, I don't know, maybe when I did it on a Shubert Fellowship in North Carolina.

Again, I'm absolutely sure that I had nothing to do with the success of *A Chorus Line.* I'm just saying it was a delightful coincidence. And, perhaps, that I was an unsung genius. Yep, that's pretty much all I'm saying.

Anyway, by the time I had written three scenes I knew we would finish the play, and about halfway through the process I knew it would be successful. I *knew* it was good. Which is weird for me. I was never positive. What the hell was happening? It was the power of the group that made everything fall into place.

Everyone seemed to have something to prove. We were all at that delicate point in our early twenties when we were looking for an experience to give us validation. This, coupled with the fearlessness that comes with youth, drove the engine of the play's creation. I'm not sure if it was fearlessness or just the fact that we hadn't been exhausted by life's disappointments yet, but I haven't known that kind of mental energy since then. The show we created was aptly titled *Feast*—and the experience of staging the play was certainly a feast for my soul.

The play was a huge hit, beyond anything I had ever imagined. After the first night, word of mouth spread

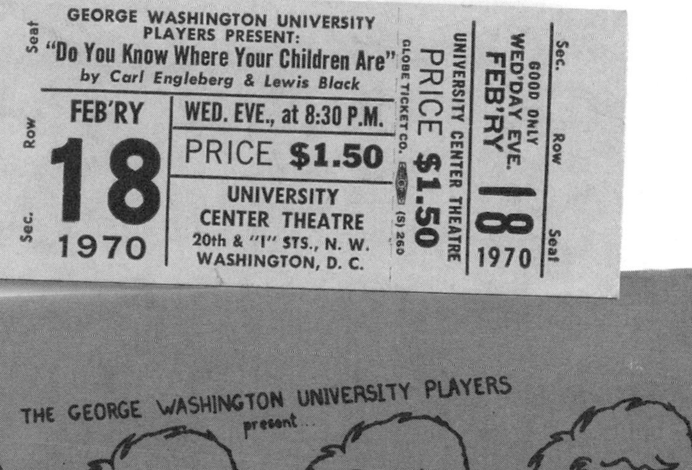
Seat
Row
Sec.
GEORGE WASHINGTON UNIVERSITY
PLAYERS PRESENT:
"Do You Know Where Your Children Are"
by Carl Engleberg & Lewis Black
FEB'RY
18
1970
WED. EVE., at 8:30 P.M.
PRICE $1.50
UNIVERSITY
CENTER THEATRE
20th & "I" STS., N. W.
WASHINGTON, D. C.
GLOBE TICKET CO. (S) 260
PRICE $1.50
UNIVERSITY CENTER THEATRE
GOOD ONLY
WED'DAY EVE.
FEB'RY
18
1970
Sec.
Row
Seat

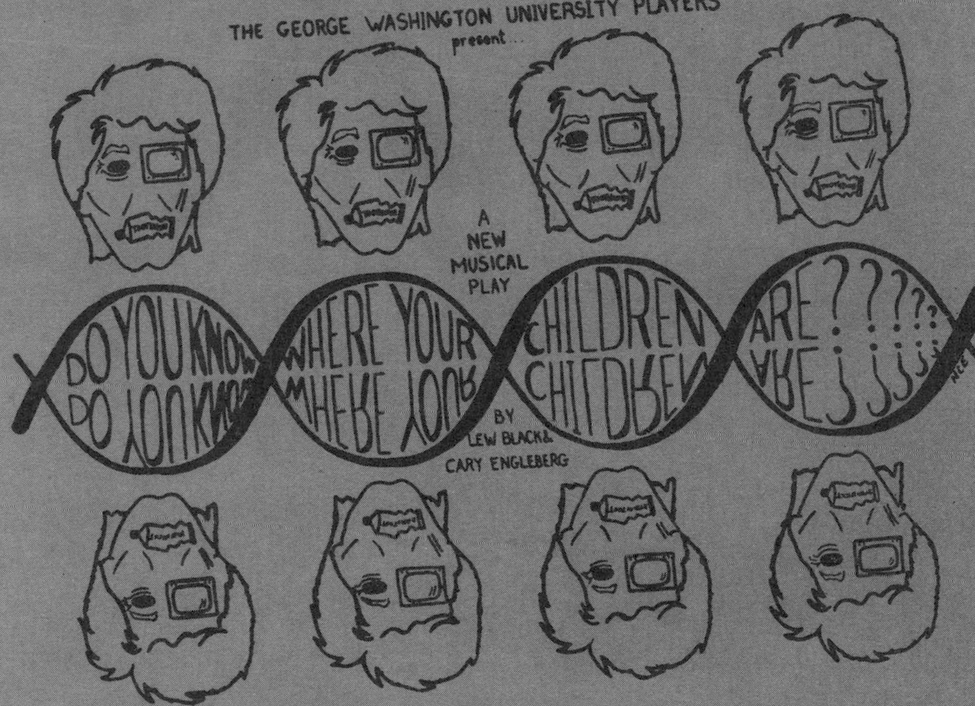
THE GEORGE WASHINGTON UNIVERSITY PLAYERS
present...
A
NEW
MUSICAL
PLAY
DO YOU KNOW WHERE YOUR CHILDREN ARE????
BY
LEW BLACK&
CARY ENGLEBERG

around campus, and the play was selling out every night. We had definitely hit a nerve. It wasn't a matter of any sort of theatrical brilliance, it was just the product of being in the right place at the right time and, of course, having a narcissistic audience hungry to stare at its own reflection.

The play centered around a young man stumbling through all the obstacles of adolescence, who then goes to college only to realize that he can't "find himself" there in the din of the late sixties and winds up leaving school. The *Raleigh News & Observer*'s chief critic gave the play a rave review. He said it was better than anything that had been done at the drama department in the last twenty years. I deeply appreciated the compliment, but I am sure it didn't sit well with my professors in the drama department—that kind of backhanded praise never does.

After the run of the play we didn't want to stop. In a few short weeks we had managed to put together a tour of North Carolina colleges with a grant provided by the North Carolina Arts Council. The cast and crew were given credits for these performances, plus we had to return to campus with a new play that spring. With the help of my friends, I learned the most invaluable lesson: You can create other ways of doing things and still participate in the society at large.

I returned to campus to meet with the temporary head of the drama department and find out my grade, as the play had been written for credit toward a master's degree. That temporary son of a bitch gave me a B. After that I permanently disliked him.

COLORADO SPRINGS

Sometimes you just have to go with the flow.

As we were preparing for the tour of *Feast,* we discovered that there was a theater for sale in Colorado Springs, Colorado. So come late January, I piled in a car with Whit Andrews, one of the actors, Jeff, the producer, and Rick Young, our technical expert, and headed out to take a look at it. We were energized by our success and driven by the feeling that we could do anything.

Driving nonstop and straight through a blizzard, we arrived at the theater, which was nestled in the foothills of Cheyenne Mountain, in a small community of ragtag houses and trailers. The theater was beautiful—set in the splendor of the Rockies and built by hand by a young man who adored theater and had died in an automobile accident. There was a wonderful feeling to the place. It couldn't have been more perfect for us—a hundred seats and built with love.

Amazingly enough NORAD, the North American Aerospace Defense Command, was located on Cheyenne Mountain. To have a theater just down the road from the entrance to the heart of our country's military industrial complex embodied the times we were living in. It was a perfect metaphor for the contrasting sensibilities of the country at the time, and life presents very few chances to live a perfect metaphor, so as a group we decided to buy it.

THE CAT'S CRADLE

It's amazing what you will do when you are too dumb to know any better.

I spent that summer in Chapel Hill having little or no idea what to do next. We had all chipped in and bought the theater but had planned to wait two years before moving out there, giving us time to raise the money to keep it, and to make sure we were all committed to the venture. After writing two plays in a year I needed a rest, and languishing in the Carolina summer heat was perfect.

Charley Huntley, one of the filmmakers who had worked on *Feast,* was the drummer for a local band. He asked me if I would like to try my hand at stand-up comedy between sets at their weekly gig at the Cat's Cradle. During the course of our tour I had become somewhat more comfortable with speaking in public since we had a question-and-answer period with the audience after each show.

Stand-up had intrigued me and I had a collection of funny stories about my sex life. Up to that point, between misinformation and my own ineptitude, my sex life had been a debacle. The Cat's Cradle was a fairly safe place to do stand-up because so many friends would be in the audience. I decided to give it a shot.

I was awful. I mean really dreadful, like scary bad. I found it much harder than the nerve-shattering experience of watching one of my plays being performed. I don't know if there is anything like standing up in front of a group of people and trying to make them laugh. Okay, sure, there's trying to remove your own gall bladder with a penknife, but besides that, I can't think of much else. And boy, was I ever trying to make them laugh. But between the dry mouth, the shakes, the vertigo, and the nausea, I was a mess.

I have a tape of the performance and I truly can't listen to more than ten seconds of it. The opening goes something like this. "Uhhhhm, welll, uhhh, I'm uhhhhhh Lewis (deep breath) Black and uhm, well, tonight, uhmmm, we are, well uhhmm, you know, uhhmmm . . ." I got some laughs, but mostly nervous ones that are caused by the tension of watching someone who doesn't know what he is doing.

John-John was onstage with me, and in a desperate attempt to get a laugh, get off the stage, and find an endless supply of beer, I put him on my lap and showed the crowd how he used his paws to masturbate. I played with his legs to show the stroking motion. We got the laugh and I hit the bar.

The funniest thing is, after all that, I went back the next week and for four weeks after that. Something about the pain of it all must have intrigued me.

Incidentally, it should be pointed out that nobody had a better time that first night than John-John. He learned a fun new trick, and, as they say, when a performer is having a good time, so will the audience. To this day I think about that evening, and when things are going south for me onstage, I find myself pondering the ethical implications of stealing John-John's act. If I didn't have so much respect for that damn dog, I just might have done it.

A REAL JOB

Well, I certainly wasn't in Oz anymore.

Since we were waiting two years to move to Colorado to start up the theater, in the fall of 1971 I returned home to Silver Spring in order to find a job. And since the one thing I understood was government work, and it was plentiful there, I figured I could find something to do . . . or just sponge off my parents for a while, like any good college graduate should.

I took the civil service exam, did quite nicely, and applied for a number of jobs in the Washington, D.C. area. The first job I was offered was with the Department of Immigration. There were two conditions, however. I would have to relocate to Arizona or New Mexico, and I would have to be willing to take instruction in the use of firearms, as my job would require me to carry a gun.

The only time I had shot a gun at anything was when I fired a BB gun at a robin. The BB bounced off his chest, and the robin looked at me as if to say, "Jesus, you are such an asshole." I quickly made up my mind—that job wasn't going to work out. Chasing a group of illegals from bumfuck town to bumfuck town across Arizona and New Mexico, armed with a pistol, was of no interest to me. Besides, I knew I would be having nightmares of a giant robin firing round after round of ammo at me.

I was also offered a job at the Appalachian Regional Commission. It looked really interesting and I accepted the position. Back then there were actual agencies established under both Kennedy and Johnson that were called—hold on to your hats, America, this might shock some of you—antipoverty agencies. Why don't we all say that together, just to get over the shock: antipoverty agencies.

You see, poverty was actually recognized as a real problem, and the government actually tried to help people overcome it. How crazy is that? What were we thinking? It was obviously a wrongheaded idea, and I am so glad that we got rid of all those agencies. Look around. Everybody seems to be doing so well, especially Appalachians who live in places called Hollers. And if they aren't doing well, let me tell you, it's their own fucking fault. Besides, I am sure they are happier not being burdened by cash, which leaves them plenty of time to whittle shit to their hearts' content.

Richard Nixon was president at the time I took the job with the ARC. People have asked me, "How could you have possibly gotten a job, feeling the way you did, working under President Nixon?" Well, the great thing about civil service is that you don't actually have to agree with the president or the party in power. Job applicants are actually picked on the basis of merit . . . hard to believe, I know. Which is why, in many ways, government agencies are not always such a terrible thing.

Sure, bureaucrats can fuck things up—which was never made more clear than when the 9-11 Commission found that the FBI and CIA computers couldn't communicate. And I am certainly not going to try and convince anyone that government is good. It's not worth it in this country—we all love our freedom, but we hate our government.

All I will say is this: The government does employ people. They were all around me when I was a kid. And it's a good thing it does. After all, for an industrial nation, we don't really make anything anymore. And one way or the other, people still have to put food on the table.

So rather than hanging around my parents' house in sweatpants all day, I was happy that the Nixon administration was willing to pay a guy like me to do whatever little I could to try to raise people out of poverty. My mom and dad especially enjoyed this notion.

It was kind of a fun time for me, chiefly because I didn't care if I was fired. That gave me a lot of freedom. I was put to work as an administrative assistant, which actually means I was a glorified secretary. But the title sounded better, like I was really doing something important.

I was assisting two women who were in charge of bringing child care centers to the women of Appalachia. For some reason, these women felt very bad for me because they thought I was overqualified for the job. Overqualified? I didn't know shit about children or care or Appalachia. Therefore, in the land of government service I was considered an expert in all three.

Anyway, they never let me type any of their work for them, which was most of what my job consisted of. They'd hand me studies to read about the children of the region or suggest that I use my time talking to people in the office to see what they were up to. I was there doing research on the commission and telling my bosses what I thought. It was fascinating.

In order to irritate those in charge, and because I was just an administrative assistant and nobody was paying much attention to me, I didn't wear a tie. Then a few weeks later they told me I had to wear one. So I would wear a tie, but I just threw it around my neck without tying it. Then they said I had to tie it—so I would tie it like you would tie a shoelace. Then they said it had to be a real knot and, finally, I relented and tied a real knot.

I think the tie allows people the possibility of being able to kill themselves at the drop of a hat. The whole death apparatus is set and ready to go—you just have to find a good firm pipe to hang from. I also think the tie is impressive to the human mind. There is a certain authority to it. "Look, he made a knot in his tie. He really must know what he's doing."

So, now that I was properly attired, just how was I going to change the lives of the poor but good folk of the Appalachian mountain range? Well, I wasn't going to change anything. There was a group of Nixon appointees within the commission, you see, who were doing everything possible to dismantle the agency. The president had given them that very mandate. Why? As far as Tricky Dick was concerned, the Appalachian region was obviously doing just great. It was a veritable boom area. Apparently it had always prospered, but the Nixon administration, in its infinite wisdom, was the first to notice.

We are talking parts of Kentucky, Tennessee, West Virginia, Virginia, and Georgia—a stretch of land that has little going for it except its hardy people and its diminishing coal mines. And that's about it. Well, it does actually have one other thing going for it—poverty stretching as far as the eye can see. To this day I take a little credit and have a modicum of pride for my contribution to that phenomenon. And if the illustrious Richard Milhous Nixon were alive today, I'd happily slap him on the back . . . of his head and scream, "What the fuck were you thinking?"

We were still floundering around in Vietnam when I was working at the commission, so President Nixon held televised news conferences at noon to keep morale high on the home front, especially among the minions who worked for the government. So we would sit at one of those long tables in a boardroom during our lunch breaks with the television set up at one end of it, and it would be just like our president was there speaking to us. There were no more than four or five of us watching him speak, the true believers and me. The rest of the commission obviously had better things to do.

I always got a kick out of listening to Nixon speak. For a guy who never seemed really comfortable in his own skin, he sure could sling the shit. At one point we were bombing the hell out of Cambodia and North Vietnam, and the president essentially said, "War is peace." You've got to love politicians—when they get on a roll they don't ever let the truth get in the way of their agenda.

When I heard the "war is peace" comment, I could not stop laughing. This really upset the true believers. They were incensed that I would laugh at their fearless leader. One guy in particular, who was—and I hate to use this word, but the guy definitely was—chubby took offense. Well, the tubby Republican stood up and challenged me to go outside and fight him.

"Yeah," I told him, "why don't we fight because I laughed at a completely idiotic statement made by your oh-so-fearless leader. Weren't you listening to what he said? Or doesn't it matter? Let's have a fistfight over a war. Now, that's smart, and let's do it on government time." So we participated in my favorite cardiovascular activity—we screamed at each other. War always brings out the best in people.

When not engaged in sociopolitical debates, I had a myriad of responsibilities. I was once assigned the job of cleaning out a closet, which was something I was more than qualified to do. When I pulled everything out, they decided that they didn't want any of it thrown out. So they had me take it thirty feet across the room and put the stuff in another closet. I spent two days of my life and the government's money moving crap from one closet to another. America was now a better place.

The great thing about being an employee of the government, and I know this irritates the hell out of a lot of people, is that it's almost impossible to get fired once you're in the job. It's really tough. I was nothing more than a pain in the ass to these folks. I'd wander from office to office, bothering them with question after question. All the questions boiled down to one: "What the hell are you people up to?" And still no one wanted to get rid of me. I don't know if I provided a certain amount of entertainment value, or if it was just too much of a hassle for them to do the paperwork. But no matter what I did, they wouldn't fire me.

During my last few weeks there I saw the budget that had been drawn up for Appalachia by the commission. Most of the budget went toward building roads. That's one way to help build an economy, but these people needed a lot more help than just highways. And why were they proposing to build these highways? To accommodate the tourists who would be flocking to Appalachia to play golf. That's right, they were planning to resurrect the economy of the Appalachian region by building golf courses.

You've got to love a country and a government that believes a poverty-stricken area could be raised from years of economic decimation by building a series of country clubs. What planet were these people living on? The whole idea was beyond belief. You might scoff at the idea of sliced golf balls crisscrossing the Appalachian landscape, but you have to be impressed with the unequivocal set of brass balls it took to come up with that plan.

I marched from office to office asking questions and making waves. "Can somebody please explain this idea to me? How is this going to work? Are you kidding me? Whose idea was this, and how come they haven't been fired? I've spent a year here only to find out that this is what you guys have been doing in closed-door meetings? You've been trying to transform Appalachia into: *Appalachia! A vacation paradise.* Are you out of your minds? Do you have any money here to hide the effects strip mining has had in the area? And I'm hardly an expert in these matters, but I'm pretty sure the sight of thousands of middle-age men in colorful polyester leisure suits ain't going to do it!"

So this was the reason our boys were dying in Vietnam, to keep this region safe for golf. I couldn't take it. I was going to have to call it quits. It wasn't for any moral reason; I was just losing my mind. And it didn't help that I was living with my parents while I worked for the government. The combination was lethal.

I learned the full nature of despair as I got fatter and fatter. I commuted by bus, an hour each way, and vowed never to commute to any job ever again. I also vowed to get the hell out of there before I became the "chubby dove" to my coworker's "chubby hawk." It was getting to the point where, if we really had been birds, we'd have fallen from the fucking sky.

I wasn't the only one who was unraveling—so was my friend Ray, who was working down at the Department of Education. The feds give a certain amount of money to school districts based on how many parents are federal employees. Ray's job was to take all of the forms sent in by the various school districts and make sure the math was correct before passing it on. That's all he had to do.

So he would spend his mornings reading the *Washington Post,* work for an hour and a half, and then go to lunch. His afternoons were devoted to reading the *Washington Star* and another hour of work, and then we would talk on the phone about how badly our days were going. He'd work no more than two or three hours a day.

After working there only a few weeks, he was pulled aside and told that he had to slow down. He'd already done in two weeks what most people in the office took six months to do. This is not an exaggeration. He said it was almost impossible to figure out how he could possibly do any less than he was already doing.

In order to stave off the misery that gripped our lives each week (well, maybe not misery so much as boredom and frustration), we would meet for lunch on Fridays at one of those salad bar and burger joints that also happened to feature all the beer you can drink. And boy did we drink. At first we would just get high, but as the weeks passed we'd find ourselves getting drunker and drunker.

Eventually we were just getting trashed and returning to work to see if anybody would notice. Nobody ever did!

In our heart of hearts we were looking to get fired, but apparently it didn't matter that we were drunk. The federal government loves everybody, especially drunks. In fact, if you check the federal tax code, I'm pretty sure there's a dry cleaning deduction in there for people who spill on themselves while enjoying a liquid lunch.

I have never enjoyed myself more in terms of people watching than when I was there. But it was the last place that I wanted to be. That year at the commission drove me away from ever seeking another job in an office. Any kind of office. Anywhere. I knew for a fact I couldn't do it; I would no doubt end up being hospitalized and electroshocked. I would have to have a complete brain fry to stay there.

They offered me another job before I left. (They wouldn't fire me, but they would give me an even better job—the mind reels.) They were going to jump me two civil service levels and give me a raise to go around establishing child care centers in Appalachia. It was a noble endeavor. But I was twenty-two years old, and I could not get over the fact that there was nobody else qualified to do this job.

I said, "I don't even have children. I can't walk into a community somewhere in West Virginia and turn to a group of mothers who have two or three kids and say, 'Well, y'all, here's how we're gonna set up the nursery!' I mean, if we are going to do this, you're going to have to find me a fake wife and a fake kid, because it sure doesn't make sense to have some twenty-two-year-old, snot-nosed college grad trying to tell a group of women who know exactly what they are doing what I think they should be doing."

And they said, "So, you want the job?"

Of course, as I'm sure you no doubt figured out, I walked away from the ARC. But as much as I hated working in that office, I still to this day believe that as much as those guys in there were screwing up, at least they were attempting to do something about a problem. I don't even think we've got offices that deal with problems like that anymore. But given time, I'm sure the government will come up with offices that will investigate offices that are supposed to look into problems. I only hope I'm here to see that day.

HOW OUR GOVERNMENT WORKS

. . . It doesn't.

Allow me to explain how our federal government works. To begin with, by the federal government I mean Democrats and Republicans working together. And the only thing dumber than a Democrat or a Republican is when those pricks work together. You see, in our two-party system, the Democrats are the party of no ideas and the Republicans are the party of bad ideas.

It usually goes something like this. A Republican will stand up in Congress and say, "I've got a really bad idea." And a Democrat will immediately jump to his feet and declare, "And I'm gonna make it shittier."

I'll illustrate. A few years ago our august body of representatives decided that a $350 billion tax cut would stimulate the economy. Well, it turned out to be a load of crap because they never know what stimulates the economy. The economy is an entity in and of itself. It goes up and down and up and down and up and down and nobody—and I mean nobody—knows why. I know this to be a fact because I took economics in college.

I would take this opportunity to explain it to you, but the truth is, I flunked economics. But it wasn't my fault. The class was scheduled at eight in the morning and there's nothing you can learn through one bloodshot eye. After I failed the first two tests, I actually grabbed the professor by the throat and screamed, "Why are you teaching this shit at this ungodly hour? Are you trying to keep it a secret?"

I never did get the answer. But I do have an answer to why a $350 billion tax cut couldn't work at that time. Because every city and every state in this country was broke. And, due to a lack of cash reserves, essential services were cut from sea to shining sea. Services like policemen—'cause you really don't need them. Services like firemen—'cause it's actually much more fun to watch stuff burn down. And, in my hometown of New York City, services like after-school programming. And, you have to trust me on this, if anybody needed to be distracted, it was those little pricks.

If you were a parent at that time, however, you had reason to count your blessings because, as part of the tax cut package, you would receive a check from the feds for four hundred dollars for every child you had. Which really paid off for those couples that had, say, a thousand kids.

Personally, I found the four-hundred-dollar-per-child rebate kind of mean. After all, all four hundred dollars does is remind people just how fucked they are. Parents would have been better off if their congressmen came to their doors and pissed on their shoes. At least that would have been a distraction.

Think about it; as a yearly tax break, four hundred dollars breaks down to less than one dollar and ten cents a day. You read that right: less than one dollar and ten cents a day! My advice to parents was to stretch that windfall by putting the kid in a box and shipping him off to one of those Sally Struthers countries where a buck ten could really do some damage. Sure, the conditions may have been a little questionable, but at least those precious little ones could have had all the dried milk they could choke down.

Instead of that tax cut, I thought the government should have initiated a public works project. In other words, pay people to build something. You see, when you employ people, they get money—and then they spend that money, and that stimulates the economy. There were—and still are—so many choices, so many places that could've used a boost. Take, for instance, Mississippi. That's a state truly in need. Be honest, have you ever heard anyone say, "Son of a bitch, I've got two weeks' vacation coming and I can't wait to see Biloxi!" I rest my case.

So all the government needed to do was send someone down there with a bag full of money, have him get off the plane, and let him walk in any direction, and he would've found a place to use it. And all he had to do was build a big fucking thing. It didn't matter what it was as long as it was big and it was a fucking thing. And then, when it was done, everybody would have gotten excited and said, "Honey, pack up the kids, we're going to see the Big Fucking Thing."

Before you knew it, the Big Fucking Thing Restaurant, the Big Fucking Thing Hotel & Casino, and the Big Fucking Thing Spa all would have sprung up around it. And then, because all of these people would have flocked to see the Big Fucking Thing, the economy would have grown.

It's not so hard to figure out. Which is why I'm thinking of running for something. Nothing local, or course. I need to run for a big fucking thing.

POLITICS AS (UN)USUAL

I never wanted to be president. It never crossed my mind.

I was born during the Truman administration, but Eisenhower is the first president that I really remember. And the sum total of those memories is that he was a World War II hero and he was married to a pleasant-enough-looking-but-hardly-beautiful woman named Mamie. The last is notable because she was the only Mamie I had ever heard of, with the exception of blond bombshell Mamie Van Doren and, of the two, never once did I pleasure myself in those formative years while thinking of anyone with the name Eisenhower.

Since then I have lived through everyone from Kennedy to two Bushes. In that time I had great hopes with Kennedy, and a little hope with Carter, and absolutely no faith in Johnson or Nixon. After all, the last two didn't seem to mind sending a lot of kids in my generation to die in a country in Southeast Asia that nobody else in the world seemed to care about. Call me crazy, but I like seeing nineteen-year-olds alive and stoned in college. It's a little quirk of mine.

Hell, Nixon even brought us Watergate, the biggest scandal ever to rock Washington. But I can't get into that right now because my nurse is on a break and I don't know where she keeps my shots. Better to be safe than sorry. And as for the esteemed Gerald Ford . . . well, he hardly registered on the political landscape—except for all the times he actually fell face-first into it. There was also, of course, Reagan and Clinton, but by then I was so disillusioned I couldn't see straight.

Given that political history, it is no wonder that I don't really like most politicians. On any level—local, state, or federal, they all pretty much suck. Especially those politicians who win. At least the losers offer "What if?" hope for years. So, in most cases, it's hard to keep hating them. But I do what I can.

Still, there was some rhyme and reason to the political process almost all the way through the Reagan administration. You could almost—almost—understand the political climate right up until then. Sure, it may have been fucked, but there still seemed to be a perverted logic to it all. Sometime in the late eighties, however, all hell seemed to break loose in Washington and, for that matter, everywhere else in this country. Within the course of a decade, crazy people just seemed to come out of nowhere. Take, for instance, H. Ross Perot.

In the nineties it finally dawned on America that with the state of the Republican and Democratic parties, we could probably use a viable third-party candidate. And to the rescue rode Texas billionaire H. Ross Perot. He probably would have been a great leader . . . if we were looking for bats in a belfry. But the guy managed to make a lot of noise in this country, and it still galls me that so many people listened to him. As far as I'm concerned, you should never listen to a guy who looks like the scary banjo kid from *Deliverance* all grown up.

But Perot wasn't the only crazy third-party politician to find his way onto a ballot. There was also Jesse Ventura. If nothing else, his election to governor proved that the citizens of Minnesota are not social drinkers. They are obviously hopeless alcoholics. But that event also points out what's great about our brand of democracy—anyone can be elected to any office. On the flip side, it also highlights what stinks about our democracy—anyone can be elected to any office.

Now, don't get me wrong. I really do believe that that kind of opportunity is awesome. But, let's be honest, he was a professional fucking wrestler right before he became governor, and I think that between wrestler and governor he really should have had to do something else. Like maybe he should have been a referee. At least that would have prepared him for budget negotiations.

Things aren't getting better, either; they're only getting worse. Arnold Schwarzenegger is the governor of California and we are not even on LSD. I don't see why people bother taking drugs anymore. When reality has become a hallucination, what do you need to hallucinate for? I was walking through the Los Angeles airport just three months after seeing Arnold in *Terminator 3,* and he was being sworn in as the governor on all the television screens. I had a nervous breakdown. I fell to my knees and I pissed and shit my pants. I was weeping and screaming for help. "What is real?" I cried out. "Can anybody tell me what is real?"

But even these guys seem to be more skillful than Vice President Dan Quayle. The name still sends the kind of chill up my spine that usually happens only after I hear, "Mr. Black, are you ready for your colonoscopy?"

Hell, who can blame me? When he was picked as Bush's running mate, he made a speech, and the second sentence out of his mouth actually was, "We must look forward to the future or *past . . . to the back.*" How would you even diagram that sentence? Let me tell you how I did it. I took out a pencil, sharpened it, and then shoved it into my right eye. It wasn't the smartest thing to do, but I sure looked jaunty in that eye patch.

But that wasn't even the worst of it. Quayle couldn't even spell the word "potato." I think the person in the second-highest office in the country should be able to spell "potato"—and I also think we should put that into the Constitution now so it never happens again. It's the simplest word in our language, and when that jackass said it out loud, he didn't realize he actually spelled the word just by sounding it out. Po-ta-to! It's right there, for God's sake. *Po-ta-to!*

Hell, a child in New Jersey spelled it correctly on the blackboard and little Danforth told him it was wrong and that he should add an "e." Jesus, how stupid can one man be? In order to save face, I think the Secret Service detail should have immediately rushed into the room, thrown Quayle to the ground, and screamed, "The vice president has been shot!" At least that would have been easier to live down than misspelling the word "potatoe."

Sadly, Quayle's stupidity disease seemed to be contagious and even morphed into a more insidious strain. In its new form, politicians were able to *spell* simple English words, they just didn't know what the words meant any longer. We all witnessed this firsthand as we watched President Clinton answer questions about his repeated trysts in the Oval Office with that big mouth, Monica Lewinsky.

Among the words for which he requested definitions were "alone" and "is." Both were equally disturbing. In the first case, it meant that if our president didn't really know what "alone" meant, he might believe the voices he was hearing in his head were actually other people.

When he followed that up with the question, "Could you tell me what you mean by the word 'is'?" I thought I would pass out. Everybody knows what "is" is. It's the first form of the conjugation of the verb "to be." And if you don't know what "is" is, you simply are not allowed "to be" the president of the United States of America. Case fucking closed!

But, of course, things got worse. When the inquisition finally got around to the blowjob questions, Clinton was in rare form. He insisted that he never lied to the American public when he assured us months earlier that he "did not have sex with that woman, Monica Lewinsky." His rationale? As he saw it, oral sex wasn't sex.

That's when I knew that he thought we had all caught the stupid disease. I look at it this way. If curling is an Olympic sport, then oral sex is sex. And even if someone is bad at it, they should still get a fucking medal.

Now we have four more years with W., as they call him, as if he were an icon. (An icon for what? Ineptitude?) Please, this guy would have made a terrific Elks Club president, and I am sure he would have done well if he were in charge of the Rotary. Hell, let's just put him in a rotary and let him go around and around and around until he's as dizzy as the rest of us are. That seems to be the only thing most of our presidents are qualified for, anyway.

Where do I begin, and when will this ever end? He has uttered banality after banality, in these most serious of times, with a self-confidence that borders on the delusional. Apparently he feels self-confidence is a substitute for intelligence. If you listen to him tell it—and I know that's a chore—he has never made a mistake. For God's sake, what more can we ask of him?

He stumbled with a purpose into a war with Iraq and had absolutely no plan for what to do afterward. And no one even called him on it until it was too late. He photo-opted himself onto an aircraft carrier just weeks after the war, appearing in front of a huge banner that read MISSION ACCOMPLISHED. The irony of it all just kills me.

W. believes that if he repeats something enough it will become the truth. I could go on for days like this, but why bother? Let me just say, he is so funny that he is not funny.

In my lifetime I have gone from John F. Kennedy to John F. Kerry, and from Dwight D. Eisenhower to George W. Bush. If that's the evolution of leadership in this country, in just a few more years we'll all be voting for plants. Which might not be so bad. After all, thanks to their ecological purpose in this world, at least plants try to clean up the air. And that would certainly be an improvement over what we've got now.

Pundits tell us we get the representatives we deserve. I have just one question for the American public. Who the fuck ran over God's dog and never bothered to apologize? I will not rest until I find you. And I will. Trust me, you cannot hide.

CORPORATE GREED

"A gold scrotum! Makes my mouth water."
—Veneer, a character in a play I wrote called *The Deal.*

Over the past couple of years we have witnessed the highest levels of corporate greed ever conceived. And the men running these companies—corporations such as Tyco and Enron and Global Crossing and Adelphia—were the greediest fuckers of the greedy. No need to look it up; it's a fact. And the word "greedy" shouldn't even apply to them. There should be a new word. It should be "piggypiggypiggyfuckpiggypiggy."

But the federal government certainly took its time to deal with those companies. Why? Because they didn't have laws in place to take action any sooner. All I have to say is this. If you don't want another Enron, here's what the law should be: If a company can't explain in one sentence what it does, it must be illegal.

And it can't be a run-on sentence either. Not a single parenthetical phrase. Not a semicolon anywhere in sight. Two commas, tops. A simple, short, declarative sentence. Just like the ones in this paragraph.

Think about this: A father and two sons ran a company named Adelphia, and one day they reached into petty cash and pulled out a billion dollars. Again, that's three people and one billion dollars—each. What were they going to do with it—start their own space program? I would have loved to be at that family meeting. "But Dad, why can't we launch our own monkeys to Jupiter? Billy and Timmy's father let them launch their monkeys to Jupiter. We hate you! You never let us do anything fun."

And how did they spend their money? Well, among other things, they took $13 million from the company and built a golf course in their own backyard. It's shocking to me that the people who worked for that company didn't rise as one and slay them. I, for one, now fully understand why the French chopped off Marie Antoinette's head.

But they're not the only ones. Dennis Kozlowski, the guy who ran Tyco, took a total of $600 million from his company. Apparently he needed to buy a lot of stuff in a hurry. "I'd like all the corn in Iowa. That's right, I'm having a hoedown."

But let's not be judgmental. He did spend a lot of that money on practical items. Like an umbrella stand. A sixteen-thousand-dollar umbrella stand, to be exact! Remember, this was a guy, a dude, not fruity in any way, but he still bought a sixteen-thousand-dollar umbrella stand.

Of course, none of us would ever think about doing that, because we all have an umbrella stand. It's called the bathtub. Let me put this into perspective once and for all. My parents spent sixteen thousand dollars on a used car. And, if they wanted, they could put a lot of umbrellas in there. They could even hop in the car and drive to where it isn't raining.

Now, I don't know about you, but if I spent sixteen thousand dollars on an umbrella stand, I would want it made out of something very special. Something that would compel me to think, "My God, I must possess this. No one else shall own it."

In a nutshell, I'd want it to be made out of Martha Stewart's vagina. Don't be so shocked. I know many of you are thinking: "But Martha Stewart doesn't have a vagina." Well, I've done the research and she definitely has one. And I hear it goes with any décor. But all of this nonsense made me stop and think. What would I do if I had $600 million? After all, these guys only bought stuff. They just acquired things in order to one-up one another, which is part of the reason things got so out of control. Let's face it, how much shit do you really need? Those guys bought art they never looked at, cars they never drove, and houses they redecorated and never lived in.

Me? If I were in their shoes, I would have been much more creative. I would have hired a young girl in her twenties and given her a remarkable salary, a generous pension plan, and the finest health insurance money could buy. Her job description? My personal ball washer.

Before you burn this book, allow me the courtesy of explaining. And rest assured that there is nothing sexual about this. I merely feel that if you're a very important man, you should have someone in front of you rinsing and scrubbing . . . rinsing and scrubbing . . . scrub, scrub . . . rinse, rinse. "I am an important CEO and my nuts should be clean."

In my dream, of course, all of the other CEOs would gather around and ask, "Lewis, who is that?" and I would reply, "Who is that? Why, that is my esteemed personal ball washer. What did you gentleman buy? Another car? Ha-ha-ha-ha-ha-ha!"

Perhaps I'm sharing too much.

THE BRICKSKELLER

You just can't fool all of the people all of the time.

Over the course of the year I spent working in D.C. for the ARC I also worked as a stand-up comedian. Don't ask me how I got the job. There was a place called the Brickskeller downtown, where folk singers would perform, playing guitar with little amplification. Sounds prehistoric, I know. These were the final moments of that era of the singer-songwriter-Autoharpist. The manager was looking for a couple of comedians and I, who had performed six times in my life, went down to audition. Apparently, with the exception of the guys on the Hill, there weren't any comedians in Washington, because I got one of the jobs.

So every other weekend, without any act whatsoever—well, I had an act, if you can call those stories about my sex life an act—I would go in and do three half-hour sets. I would tell the story of "The Ascent of the Left Breast to the Nipple" or "Sexual Education as Taught by My Gym Teacher Through Sex Ed Films" or "Trying to Lose My Virginity to the Girl Who Didn't Know Where It Was Supposed to Go." Those semiprepared sets were bad, but my backup set was even worse. I would talk about what happened at the office that week, or about how I felt about the government. You really shouldn't be winging it when you aren't very good. The audience gets mad when you are neither comfortable onstage nor that funny.

Watching me try and light a cigarette while I was onstage was terrifying at best. It would take me a good minute and a half to get the shaking cigarette to the shaking match. But for some reason, I kept going back. Any sane person would have called it a day. I was always in a panic when I stood up in front of a crowd or just a few people. It always scared the shit out of me.

Learning to be a comic is like learning to be a boxer with your hands tied to your sides. You just take hit after hit, and while you are getting pummeled, you figure out, *Wow, if I just did this, I wouldn't get hit.* Then you get hit again. I was knocked out a lot that year. But I learned a lot. I learned I would probably not be much of a comic.

A LIFE IN THE THEATER

"It's a Colorado Rocky Mountain high."
—John Denver

Any doubts I may have had about pursuing a life in the theater were erased by just one year of working for the federal government. I decided to live without a net to avoid choking on that net by the age of fifty. Watching my father drop out of his career in sea mine engineering certainly was a major influence on my decision, that and the fact that I really didn't cope well in an office environment. It was time to head to Colorado Springs and see if it was going to be a dream or a nightmare.

Even though the group had decided to wait two years after buying the theater to move out there, a number of us decided to head out early. As I was making my way west with a couple of friends, John Denver's "Rocky Mountain High" came on the radio. It was the first time I had ever heard it. It was a song extolling Colorado. I turned to my friends and yelled, "We're *fucked*! *We are fucked!* Are you listening to this? Every asshole in America is going to move to Colorado. And the saddest thing is, we are the first of those assholes. And you know what's worse? This John Denver guy will probably be there too. *We are fucked!*"

Colorado Springs was one hell of a mix of people. We knew nothing of the demographics before we got there. If we had, it just may have influenced our instinctive decision. There were the folks from NORAD. There were the soldiers of Fort Carson, which was the military base where the first experiments were taking place on how to create an all-volunteer army. They brought in every possible stoner and misfit to try and find out what it would take to get them to stay in the army. And what were the results of this study? Well, at eleven o'clock at night the kitchens would pump out pizzas, affectionately called NORAD pizzas. "Let's see . . . it's eleven at night, hmm; oh, I get it. You guys are stoned, so here, how about some free pizza." That's how you keep an ever-vigilant army—the promise of a piping-hot pepperoni pizza.

There was also a whole group of people who thought they were cowboys. Actually they were more like shitkickers, if you will. They'd work in offices and wear cowboy hats on the weekend. In short, this is the kind of town it was: One of the first headlines that we read in the local paper upon our arrival was written in bright red—COMMIE BIGWIG COMES TO TOWN. Not that I have a big ego, but I took that notice personally. I was also paranoid. After all, I hadn't told anybody when I was arriving.

In addition to the townies, there were the students and faculty of Colorado College. It was a camp for rich kids whose main interest seemed to be skiing. All told, it was an extraordinarily mixed bag in which theater had almost no place. But that didn't matter to us. We had a dream; therefore, we were oblivious to the facts. That was a good thing and a bad thing—good in that we were steadfast and resolute, bad in that we probably shouldn't have been there.

The great metaphor for our times that had drawn us to this place on our fist trip out there was going to work against us. Theater can't compete with a giant military complex located in the middle of a mountain, and it certainly can't compete with shit-kickers. For those of us in the theater, talking about how wonderful it is and how it can change people keeps us going. But when you are sitting between one of the largest military bases in the country and America's first line of defense headquartered in a mountain, we had to be deaf, dumb, and blind to think this was going to work. We needed at least five hundred years of theater to change the people in this town. But the pizza was tasty.

Oblivious, we set about our task. We did improvisation performances wherever we could, including the army base's coffee houses. (Yep, they had coffee houses at Fort Carson, and speakers such as Jane Fonda.) I also wrote a children's play that we performed around the city, and we did a production of John Guare's *House of Blue Leaves*. The irony, of course, is that we couldn't do any of these shows in our own theater because we didn't have the proper zoning permits. The gentleman who built the theater was given dispensation to use the space, as he was a native son. But we were outsiders, interlopers; we might as well have been Yankees in the South after the Civil War.

We presented a play that summer in the park at the center of town, called *Rejoice: A Simple Song*. The park, it turns out, was avoided by most of the community. It was where the local drug addicts hung out. This didn't faze us. We had no choice. We had no theater. We were actually living in our theater at that point. So we put on shows in the park for smallish audiences. It was a very sophomoric piece of work on my part, but it had some wonderful music and dance and a wonderful set. It wasn't an overwhelming success, except that we had done it, and that was an accomplishment in and of itself.

We took it to Fort Carson, Colorado College, and the prison in Cañon City. If you ever want to know what it's like to do drugs, just present a play, any play, at a prison—and make damn sure there are women in the cast. The response to the play had absolutely nothing to do with the words that were uttered or the actions displayed. The prisoners were seeing breasts, and breasts informed their interpretation of what they were watching. Hell, they could have been looking at Lady Macbeth crawling around on the floor screaming, "Out, out damn spot!" and all they would have thought was, "She sucks as a housekeeper, but look at those tits! Get over here and clean me, Lady—I'm dirty!!!"

All of the productions helped us get by. And we were doing what we had come there to do, whether anyone was paying attention to us or not. As it turned out, one man in particular was paying attention, the vice principal of the local high school and a former marine. He liked our vision, and we established ourselves as the school's theater company in residence. We desperately needed a base where our actors could spend time practicing their craft. It was obvious after our summer show that we needed time to grow and that we weren't going to be able to sell a lot of theater out there.

So we performed in any classroom that would have us, from algebra to history. We would do scenes from plays that the students were reading, and we even directed a student production of *A Midsummer Night's Dream.*

We also held discussions and led theater games at the prison, which is like working at an insane asylum—everyone is paranoid and everyone has an agenda. Spending time with the inmates was always edgy and a little weird, yet somehow fulfilling. I know for a fact that it was fulfilling for them, because I was the only guy from our group that came to the prison—the rest were women. This no doubt helped, because the guys would pay attention—they *really* paid attention. They would even listen to me—and I didn't have tits.

We continued to do shows at Fort Carson at the coffee houses, and I did a lot of stand-up at the base. One night, while rolling in for a show there, I smoked just a couple of puffs of the herb—marijuana, if you will. Every so often, marijuana has a tendency to overwhelm the senses and render you catatonic. And this was one of those nights.

I spent the first five minutes of my act thinking I was speaking aloud when in fact I wasn't saying anything at all. I would think my lines, and then a few moments later I would say aloud, "You get it?" Then I would laugh bemusedly in response to nothing. And every now and then I would babble an incoherent fragment from a story I thought they were hearing. My friends kept pointing at their mouths, trying to convey my near muteness. At first I just thought they were telling me to hurry up because they were hungry and wanted to go get a bite, but eventually I figured it out.

When I heard it on tape, I couldn't believe it. People will listen to practically anything, as long as you act like you know what you are doing. George W. Bush and Dan Quayle are masters at this. They both launch into nonsense and never flinch at the words they are uttering. I guess that would require them to actually listen to themselves, but no such luck.

Despite lapses like my mute comedy bit at the base, however, we actually got to the point where we were functioning on all cylinders and had made ourselves a presence in the community. The problem was that we were all very young (nobody was over twenty-two) and there wasn't another major theater within miles of us. We had absolutely no one to turn to for guidance except the vice principal, and the group suffered a long, slow meltdown.

There were four newlywed couples among us, who were not only trying to come to grips with their new marriages, but were also living in a commune, which certainly didn't help the process. Why would anyone live in a commune, you might ask? Well, it's a place where people live and work together to accomplish a common goal . . . and because they are broke. We had three houses at the end of a road that we lived in together, and we were always on top of one another. We even had five chickens because, back then, you could have chickens in Colorado Springs, or at least no one seemed to care about ours. That was one of the few advantages to living in the Wild West. We probably could have had a herd of fucking cattle down there if we'd wanted.

Anything went in those days. And if we'd worn cowboy hats, the theater might still be there today.

NIXON VS. MCGOVERN

"When the going gets weird, the weird turn pro."
—Hunter S. Thompson

In November of 1972 we all cast our votes for George McGovern, in hopes that the candidate representing peace would win. We were completely oblivious to the onslaught that would take place. Somehow we had managed to completely insulate ourselves from the reality that surrounded us. Folks in the theater are good at that.

A bunch of us sat down with a case of beer to watch the election returns. It soon became quite evident that Nixon was going to win in a landslide, and this depressed us to no end. So we started really knocking back the beers. We were in shock. I don't know how it happened, but we decided that if the state you came from went to Nixon, you had to pee on the television. We placed a plastic mat under it and spent a good part of the evening drinking and peeing. Ineffectual as it was, it made us feel better and helped express a rage that was simmering in all of us. You sure feel a sense of alienation when you find out the rest of the country is thinking in a way totally different from how you are.

By the time McGovern had conceded and Nixon was giving his acceptance speech, I was extremely trashed and extremely upset. So I did the only thing I could do to express my feelings of loathing and outrage. I took a shit on the television set. That's right. It's not something I look back on with pride, but it made plenty of sense then—especially considering the condition I was in.

My friends, who were definitely as far gone as I, cheered me on. While Nixon spoke, I rubbed the shit across his televised face. No doubt these actions were the expression of a mind that had not yet properly matured, but I got a strange sense of satisfaction doing it while we watched the shithead speak. It was pretty disgusting, but at the time it was also pretty funny.

I have never done anything like that since and I'm sure I never will again. And not because I have matured so much that I would find it inconceivable. It's just that we now have remotes and, if that kind of urge hit me, I would merely change the channel. Besides, I now own a much more expensive television and there are certain things you just don't fuck with.

STAND-UP AT THE MAX

Riotous comedy

A few months later we were performing an improvisational show at the prison in Cañon City and I was to open with a stand-up comedy routine. I was still extremely ill equipped in the craft of comedy, and I certainly had little or no sense of how to control an audience. I wasn't doing it often enough to really be learning it.

A few minutes into my act I said to the crowd that it amazed me that they were all locked up while President Nixon, with the Watergate scandal looming larger every day, was not only enjoying his freedom but was still the president. Apparently this struck a nerve, the inmates went wild, their laughter was quickly followed by anger, and within a minute or two they were at a fever pitch. They were smashing chairs and shouting curses, and they seemed to be moving into riot mode. My meager attempts to calm them were of no avail, and the guards quickly escorted us out of there.

That was the last time they let us perform at the prison. I was glad. I thought maybe I could come back some day when I knew what I was doing.

In the spirit of the tell-all, full-disclosure book, however, I must admit that this was not the only time I ended up behind bars. Many years later I agreed to participate in a publicity stunt for the New York-based radio show *Opie and Anthony,* which did not end happily.

Along with another comic named Jim Norton, I was asked to ride around Manhattan in an all-glass bus filled with topless teenage strippers. Our assignment was to report back, via remote, to hosts Opie and Anthony about what was going on inside the bus and what kinds of reactions this extravaganza was inciting among the people outside the vehicle.

It was all fun and games until the bus got too close to city hall, where then-President Clinton was scheduled to appear. The powers that be in the city government didn't think this spectacle was very funny, despite our insistence that nobody on the face of God's green earth would enjoy the sight of teenage titties more than the president. The argument fell on deaf ears.

Everyone on the bus was arrested, and we were held in a city jail for more than twenty-four hours before being released without a single charge filed against us.

After that little foray in the system, I can now confidently tell you that jail really sucks. And, despite the advances made in such institutions since my visit to the Cañon City prison, the entertainment on the inside hasn't gotten any better either.

ROCKY MOUNTAIN SIGH

Your dream may be exquisite, but eventually you have to wake up.

There are dreams and then there is reality. We had pursued our dream, but it only took us so far. Understandably we had become more and more concerned with our individual goals. As much as we might have accomplished, we were out of our depths—the more we worked, the more we understood what we needed to do, and the more impossible it seemed to be.

So we put the theater up for sale. We had a number of interested buyers, and initially it looked as if we might get our investment back. No such luck. The old west has its ways, and all our neighbors had to do to prevent the sale was not grant water rights to the buyer—water rights, as in access to water that crosses their land. So our friendly neighbors squeezed us and we got back a pittance. The loss of money wasn't as tough to deal with as the fact that we all spun out in different directions, knowing full well we would never know another time like this in our lives. It was time to deal with the real world, and that's a lot easier to do as a group.

I was offered a job by the vice principal of the school running the vocational educational program for the county. I deeply appreciated the fact that he had that kind of faith in me, but I didn't want any kind of real job in the first place, so it made no sense for me to stay on. I couldn't see trying to get kids interested in working in places where I wouldn't want to work.

Fuck Horace Greeley, it was time for me to head back east.

THE UPPER PENINSULA

Where one goes when one wants to become an alcoholic.

I spent that summer helping my friend Ray's dad build a log cabin in the Upper Peninsula of Michigan. A land completely unto itself, it is like another country, inhabited by the ancestors of Scandinavians who obviously wanted to find a place that was as bleak and barren during the winter as the place they left. It's absolutely beautiful in the summer, and then the rest of the year it resembles a freezer that needs to be defrosted. Drinking is the main activity there.

We built the cabin overlooking Lake Michigamme. I know it might seem strange to imagine me in the middle of the woods building a cabin; well, that's because it is. But it was good to get away from the world, and the Upper Peninsula is as far away as you can get without leaving the country. Once we had the concrete slab in place, every day we would bring up the television to watch the Watergate hearings. They were finally closing in on President Nixon and his cronies. It was spectacularly surreal to watch John Dean's testimony on a television in the middle of beautiful white birches overlooking a serene lake while putting up logs. If that's not what America is all about, I don't know what is.

The strangest thing that summer was that I kept hearing

babies crying at night in the cabin I stayed in by myself. I hate to relate the following, because antiabortionists will just love this story, but I discovered that the cabin had been used in the early 1900s by a veterinarian who performed abortions for the townspeople there.

My summer confirmed a suspicion I'd always had. Weird things happen in the woods.

THE YALE SCHOOL OF DRAMA

College prepares you for the real world. Graduate school prepares you for an even realer world.

I had made my way back east and spent a year as a playwright-in-residence in a small theater just outside Silver Spring. As much as I had no concept of what I was doing as a stand-up comic, as a playwright I still had just as little. And after working in that theater for a year, I had begun to fully realize my limitations. That's when I decided it was time to get a master's.

College is the place you go when you don't want to do shit. It's a place to hide until you figure things out. And while it's important to actually be interested in the subject you are studying, it is mainly an opportunity to get away from society in general and continue to pursue your interests in what is most certainly not the real world.

Don't ask me how, because I will never know, but I got into the Yale School of Drama, which is about as far away from the real world as you can get outside of living on LSD. It was here that my tolerance for authority began to break down for good. I entered the school believing that students had established a voice in their academic affairs. It was one of the few palpable accomplishments of the sixties. Well, that may have been true for a portion of the academic community, but this was a drama school—an Art school with a capital A, and those don't count.

The brochure for the school stated that my relationship to my teachers there would be that of apprentice to master. When I read that I couldn't stop laughing. Wow, the last time I heard that word used was in "The Sorcerer's Apprentice." I couldn't believe one of the best schools in the country was espousing a medieval model of education. I might have saved myself some mental anguish had I known they would take it so literally.

One of my professors actually stood up the first day and explained how the apprentice-master dynamic worked. I raised my hand and said, "You know, if we were really going to apprentice, shouldn't we apprentice to a plumber or something? At least we'd be making $15.95 an hour. I realize you guys are artists. But you know, if you were making real money at it, I don't think you'd be taking on apprentices."

Needless to say, I wasn't very popular with that guy after that.

I went to Yale much the same way that the rest of my generation went to Vietnam. Only I was the one who was going to be saved. Talk about rose-colored glasses. I entered those ivy-covered walls filled to the brim with idealism. I thought I would go there and sit by the still waters, listening as they opened the world of drama and a life in art to me. Well, that wasn't the way it was. It would have been just as easy for me to have tried to become a Catholic priest.

As our first semester came to a close, a group of us, mostly playwrights, were having lunch. The school had mandated that January was to be a work month. There would be no classes and we would work on special projects of our own devising, working behind the scenes on upcoming theatrical productions. We were in the midst of an energy crisis and in order to conserve, the school would shut down for the month.

This was 1975. And since then we have done nothing, I mean, squat, zilch, nada, to deal with our energy problems. Except for some insanity that Cheney came up with, which Senator McCain eloquently called "the no lobbyist left behind" bill. There has been no action taken by any of our leadership at any time to protect the interests of the American people. It has all been about the needs of Big Oil.

For Christ's sake, this has got to be simple at this point, hasn't it? Oil is like heroin and we are the addicts. And our government is obsessed with protecting the pusher. What about solar fucking energy, for God's sake? Why not? Because the sun burns and oil soothes. The sun goes away each day and it doesn't tell you where it's going, and oil generally lies around long enough to get you and your car where you're going. The mind reels with the greed and stupidity our leadership has shown in regard to energy. The American public is nothing more than a toilet seat. But I digress. . . .

So, we were discussing what we were going to do while we helped conserve our nation's vital resource, when an actor sitting with us asked our opinion of a suggestion made to him by a speech teacher of what he should do during the month. He was told he had a problem with a sibilant *s*. And since Yale's hospital was one of the finest in the world, and we as students of the university had an extraordinary health plan, it might behoove him to have his jaw broken and reset during that month in order to correct the problem. This poor kid was so twisted around that he was actually considering it.

I was utterly in shock. I couldn't believe it. A sibilant *s*? I thought that was something you could sort of work through. Couldn't he just spend the month, maybe two hours a day, working on his pronunciation? *Break his fucking jaw?* I walked out of there immediately, saying, "If you let them break your jaw, I will break your fucking leg." And I went down to see the dean of students, with whom I'd already become enamored because he'd begun discussing the fact that they were thinking of throwing me out of school. I had a tendency to tell the faculty at every turn, in so many words, basically that they were full of shit. But this was really off the charts.

"You're going to break the kid's jaw?" I said. "You can't have teachers doing that, all right? I don't know if you have some sort of Geneva Accord thing here, but in the outside world, we're not considered prisoners of war! You can't talk to apprentices like this! And if you're not going to stop it, I'll go talk to the guy myself."

It was a constant battle pretty much my entire three years there. They would talk about how something in the program that they wanted to do for us couldn't happen, and I would raise my hand and say, "You know, Plymouth gives out a thousand-dollar rebate if you buy one of their cars. I think the student body would be more than happy to let you remove whatever programs you want, as long as you can give us some money back." None of this went over well.

I can recall yet another stunning moment in the Yale School of Drama out-of-body experience. There was a woman in my class who had very large breasts, the kind that would make Dr. Phil recommend a breast reduction. And if the procedure were around at that time, I'm sure some irresponsible teacher would have directed her to the hospital and asked to be present for the surgery.

She approached me one day and asked if I had ever heard of a breathing exercise whereby the professor sits on your chest while you are speaking to teach you something about breath control. Apparently, the teacher had sat on her breasts. I went around and asked all the other kids in the class if the teacher had sat on their chests as well. The whole concept of sexual harassment didn't really exist at that time, and sitting on a woman's breasts wasn't so much sexual harassment as it was abusive. And so I went back to the dean's office yet again. I spent a lot of time there.

GOING TO THE CHAPEL

And the Lord spoke unto Lewis . . . but it was too late.

Since my head was in a continual spin cycle at the drama school, it made perfect sense that I would get married at this time. The wedding took place at the courthouse in Rockville, Maryland, with just my immediate family and hers. Directly following the ceremony my brother and I walked out the door just as two officers of the law were passing by with a prisoner shackled between them. I looked at my brother and said, "When God sends you a message he certainly makes it loud and clear."

The marriage was finished in less than a year.

THREE YEARS OF HELL

"I saw some of the best minds of my generation destroyed by madness."
—Allen Ginsberg

The administration at Yale tried to throw me out of school, using as a line of reasoning that I obviously wasn't satisfied there; it was true, but I had nowhere else to go, nor did I really want to go to any other school. As much as I was losing my mind, I knew I was in the right place for me. I was sure there were much better ways to teach theater, but I was learning in spite of the teachers. It made no sense to transfer to another school since this one was considered the best.

I was told I wasn't writing enough, but I knew I had written as much as my classmates. So I told them if they tried to throw me out I would go to the *New York Times* and expose the insanity I was witnessing daily. They didn't expel me and I chose to stay.

I was given the opportunity to work with some of the finest young artists in the American theater, who were surrounded by some of the biggest asshole teachers I've ever come across in my life. I'd never watched a group of people come in to a place with so much energy, and watch that energy sucked out of them so fast. Three months into our training and we were a group of walking wounded who really never recovered.

Every time I think about that place, I inevitably start to limp.

TOAD'S PLACE

Comedy 101

I stayed on in New Haven for two more years because I wasn't ready to move to New York. I was also broke and could live on the cheap in New Haven, which was one of the few reasons to actually live there. In my search to keep myself afloat, I decided to try to become the emcee at Toad's Place, an aptly named rock and roll club just off campus that was frequented by people who seemed to have climbed out from under rocks. I still wasn't much of a stand-up, but I'd gotten to a place where I was at least comfortable with my own pain. The manager told me I was the first comic who had wanted to work there. It would soon become apparent why.

I first went onstage there on a night that he was auditioning punk and rock bands. I brought at least fifteen friends with me so there would be some friendly faces in the front row that I could turn to in my hour of need. We watched as punk band after rock band after punk band pounded the walls of this joint with their music. There were also about ten arcade games off in the corner of this cavernous space that were making noise.

The room was nearing the far reaches of chaos, when the manager approached me and said that I was next. He also kindly pointed out a group of guys sitting to the left of the stage that I shouldn't tangle with. I was glad to be forewarned. That's just the kind of comforting news I needed to hear before I walked onstage. The room was still resounding with the din of screaming guitars, as if all the sounds the bands had made remained in the air. I could barely hear my own thoughts, which were scattershot at best.

The manager introduced me, his voice barely audible as he whispered into an offstage mike. "Next up is a guy who is really interesting—I think you'll like him. We have never had anyone like him here, so it should be fun. And he says he's sort of funny. Lewis Black." No one heard a thing because most of them were talking or playing pinball or recovering from the sonic boom of the last band that had no doubt loosened a filling or two. I looked out at the audience. They seemed prehistoric. Like dinosaurs, they moved about slowly with bloodshot eyes, faces glazed from an overdose of sound. These people weren't even able to hear yet.

Silence is an absolute necessity when it comes to doing comedy. It's in silence and the ensuing tension of it that the laugh is born. Even just a vague bit of quiet helps. But no such luck. So I launched into my set. What difference did it make? No one was paying attention except for my friends.

I told a story that I had done a number of times before, about my sexual ignorance in high school. One of the guys in the gang I'd been warned about asked me where I had gone to high school. I told him, and that seemed to calm them down. I had enough on my plate just trying to tell the story, let alone worrying about getting laughs, which seemed out of the question since the pinball wizards had resumed going full tilt around the room. I was just looking to stand my ground and be on my way. From stage right I began to hear the voice of a young woman. No one in the room could hear her, except a few of my friends.

"What's the matter with you? What's the matter with you?" she shot at me. "You got a problem, buddy? You got some kind of problem? You got a problem with your dick? Is that it? You got a pecker problem? I bet you got a small dick, a little teeny tiny dick. I bet if I came up there and pulled your pants down we couldn't even see your dick, that's how small it is."

She was relentless. I just kept trying to get through my story, because there was no way I could really let the audience in on what was happening. They didn't care, anyway. They were too busy drinking and waiting for the next band. Out of the corner of my eye, I noticed that she was walking toward the stage, telling me that my dick was as tiny as a dick could be. Too bad my mother wasn't in the audience to inform her about my "big crotch."

Anyway, when she made it to the stage, she stood directly in front of me and screamed at the top of her lungs, "You're not talking about boobs, you're talking about breasts!"

So that was it. The word "boobs," a throwback to my days in high school, is what had set her off. I looked into her eyes, and she seemed to be high on speed. I could tell because there were white lines running down the middle of her pupils. Her screaming stunned the room into attention. Then she pulled up her blouse and exposed herself first to me and then to the rest of the room. Everything came to a screeching halt, as the dinosaurs stopped and slowly turned their heads. You could almost hear the creaking of their necks. The back of the room had a wall of windows, and even passersby had stopped to take a gander. Apparently two teats can stop anything. She stood her ground for five beats so that everyone could get a good look, and then angrily stomped off the stage.

The room had gone from chaos to utter silence. We had finally arrived at a perfect comic moment. I had the audience's complete attention, and the tension in the room was as high as it could possibly get. All I had to do was release the tension by waiting three beats and then say anything, I mean anything, and there would be a huge laugh. I could say "tuna fish" or "spiky teasel" or "farty bo bo"—it didn't matter. In my brain, the little performer in my head had already gone to the dressing room and was sipping a Jack Daniel's on the rocks; he was finished.

I decided that when the moment was right I would simply thank my sister for joining me onstage for my big finish. Then I would go on to say how great it was to be at Toad's Place and how it would be even greater not to ever come back. But just as I was getting ready to speak (and this is no exaggeration, I am not making this up), a gentleman in the back of the house leaps onto a table and shouts out, "Ladies and Gentlemen, I am a faggot and I brought this girl here this evening. I think I deserve a round of applause."

The entire audience turned and applauded him, and they then turned back to me. The difficulty I was having at this point is that with the applause, all the tension in the room evaporated. I was now going to have to build the tension back up, but how do you top two breasts and a gay caballero?

"Ladies and Gentlemen," I said. "I am thrilled that my brother and sister could join me here for the finale of my act. It's been a pleasure. Thank you and good night." There was a pause, and from the back of the room the manager cried out, "Jesus Christ, that's some of the best stuff I've ever seen. Keep going."

Keep going? The man was a fucking sadist.

But I did keep going. I don't know what I was thinking, maybe that I could salvage the set. The dinosaurs went back to grazing, and my set ended with a whimper. It struck me later that I may not have known if I was ever going to be a good comic, but if I could have that kind of effect on at least one person in the room then I might be on the right track.

Apparently I had the right instincts. Not very long ago, as I was winding my way to the end of a show at the Punchline in Atlanta, a heckler felt I was being too hard on Vice President Cheney. He informed me in no uncertain terms that the vice president was serving his country, and asked what was I doing for my country.

I paused and said, "I do this. This is what I do."

Unlike my first night at Toad's Place, I was much better prepared to answer that gentleman. By then I knew who I was as a comic. That was hardly the case back in the day when dinosaurs still roamed the room in New Haven.

And, looking back, the sad thing was I kept going without a prayer of being successful; but I couldn't stop myself. I believe that is one of the signs of a true comic—once you've dug a hole deep enough to bury yourself, and you still try to get out with all that dirt going into your mouth, even when you have no chance of survival, and you think it's fun. I've always thought it was fun. When you can stand onstage and watch yourself die and enjoy every second of it, believing that you can get the audience back when there isn't a chance in hell, that's when you understand the ancient expression: Death is easy, but comedy is hard. Like most of the comics I know, I am not an altogether healthy person.

AUDITIONING TO BE ME

Be all that you can be, and it still may not be enough.

About ten years ago, a good friend of mine, Joy Behar, got a deal to tape a pilot for her own sitcom. She was going to play a high school principal, and I was going to play a history teacher who had a tendency to go off on rants in front of his students. I realize it seems like a stretch, but I was pretty sure I could handle it.

Anyway, these people from Hollywood came to New York and watched me perform at Catch a Rising Star, a great club on the Upper East Side that's no longer around. The writer, director, and producer all thought I was great. And I know this because after my performance they came up to me and said, "Lewis, you were great." People from Hollywood are known to do that sort of thing.

Well, they went back to the West Coast armed with a tape of my act, which they wanted to study in order to get "a sense of me as a character." I thought things were looking good for me and, true to their word, I received a script from them two weeks later. They even called me to ask what I thought of it.

Well, what else was I going to think? The script featured a character named "Lewis" and every word the character "Lewis" said in the script were words I, the real

Lewis, had already said two weeks earlier onstage. I told them the only thing that came to mind.

"I love it! This 'Lewis' character is great! Can't wait!"

That's when things got a little surreal. That's when they told me that CBS was ready to fly me out to the West Coast in order to audition me for the role of Lewis. That's right, they were going to make me audition to play me!

This didn't make me overwhelmingly happy, but considering I was somewhat underemployed at the time, I got on the plane. And during the flight I realized, for the first time in my life, why I had taken LSD in my youth. It was the only drug that could have ever prepared me for the moment when I would be auditioning to be myself.

Things got a little weirder once I hit the tarmac at Los Angeles International Airport. The writer, director, and producer took me off to a place where I could rehearse. Apparently they thought that during the flight—what with the airline food and flying through all of those time zones—I might have turned into someone else.

So I rehearsed. And then I rehearsed some more. And when the Trinity of Tinseltown was convinced that I was as good at being me as I could possibly be, they brought me to CBS to audition for the network.

To be perfectly honest, it was probably the best audition I have ever had. I thought I was really good at being me—and let's face it, if I didn't feel that way, I belonged in a hospital somewhere. Thank God I was cognizant enough to remember that when you're auditioning to be yourself, the one thing you have to bring to the table is a little fucking self-confidence. You can't stand there thinking, "Am I me? Am I *really* me?"

I knew from my years in theater that in order to nail

this audition, I needed to commit to being me. Well, I gave it my best shot, and I scored. They laughed, they cried, they shook my hand, and they even said, "Oh, man, you're going to hear from us!"

And I did. A couple of hours later they called to inform me that while I was a pretty damn good me, they had auditioned a couple of other actors and found one who was a really terrific me. Apparently there are actors out there who spend their lives training to become other people and one of them had become a better me than I could have imagined myself being.

Well, as they say, that's show business. And I'm over it. I really am. I hardly think about it anymore. Still, there are a couple of questions that nag at me. What the fuck did that other guy know about me that I didn't know? And where did I fail myself?

I may never know the answers. But I do know the pilot was never picked up for a series and thank God for that. Imagine having people on the street approaching you and saying, "You know, you kind of remind me of that Lewis guy on television—except he's just a little bit better. Can I have *his* autograph?" My life is complicated enough. I don't need that shit.

THE END

And on the eighth day, God created Starbucks as far as the eye can see, and he said, "Give me venti cappuccino—I am exhausted."

I have traveled extensively across this country and, lately, around the world, and I have made an extraordinary discovery. A discovery about something that philosophers and the great thinkers of this or any other time have been pondering for centuries. Most of them have come to the same conclusion. They have looked to the heavens and believed that the universe, as we know it, ends somewhere out there in space.

Well, I'm here to tell you, they were all mistaken. I have seen the end of the universe and it's right here on Earth. Right here in this country, as a matter of fact. Right in Houston, Texas, to be exact.

It was a shocking epiphany. I left a comedy club one day and walked to the end of the block, and there, on one corner, was a Starbucks. A rather common sight, to be sure. But across the street in an office building that was a mirror image of the structure holding the Starbucks . . . stood another Starbucks.

At first I looked back and forth, convinced the sun was playing tricks on my eyes. I thought, let me look at *this* Starbucks, and when I turn around, there couldn't possibly be a Starbucks behind me. After all, I reasoned, if there was a just and loving God, he certainly wouldn't allow this shit to happen. So I turned slowly, convincing myself that when I opened my eyes, I would see a Denny's or a Gap or even a Mobil station.

But I didn't. It was indeed true. I was looking at a Starbucks across the street from a Starbucks. Things went fuzzy for a moment, but when my head cleared, it felt as if God had reached down and bestowed upon me all the knowledge ever gathered since the beginning of time. I was indeed looking at the much-sought-after end of the universe.

Since then I have been roaming the countryside spreading the word. But still people persist in asking, "Lewis, tell us, how do you know?" And I tell them, "Go there. Stand between those two Starbucks and look at your watch. Time will actually stand still." And then they go. And they know.

Since my discovery I have witnessed things that have no explanation other than that the end is closer than we think. An idiot has been reelected to the highest office in the land, and the Boston Red Sox have won the World Series. The latter, especially, was truly pivotal, and the world will never be the same again. I may be crazy, but I believe it's as biblical a moment as we could have.

However, there are still those who continue to doubt. Much like the controversy that continues to swirl around the Kennedy assassination, the questions linger. Chief among them is this one: "Lewis, are there perhaps too many Starbucks franchises?"

The answer, sadly, is self-evident. Yes. When a man stands in a Starbucks, steaming cup of coffee in hand, looking out the window at an empty storefront across the street and declares, "Honey, we're mortgaging the house, for I see a future filled with delicious and overpriced mochaccino," that's it. Game fucking over.

That is definitely the end. And it is written here.

THE ENDING

With much gratitude to the reader who has made it this far.

Americans continue to rapidly homogenize ourselves into a neutered oblivion. For a country founded on the protection of the unique, we relish our sameness. Even I, in my travels, find a completely idiotic solace when I enter a mall; there is something soothing about it. I reach a trancelike state that can't be healthy, can it? Of course it can't—of that much I am certain.

We maul all the threads of the grand international fabric we should be—Italy becomes the Olive Garden, Ireland becomes Applebee's, France is transformed into a Starbucks. Apparently there is no profit in the unique, or not enough to make it worthwhile to preserve. Ultimately it drains the life out of us, and existentialism starts to make more and more sense. How could Sartre truly understand existentialism if he never drove through Ohio from one Wendy's to the next?

This is reflected in those who become our authority figures. The unique to them is nothing more than disturbing. There is never any time for questions because they have no answers. It's best to keep one's mouth shut if one intends to move up in this world. I can't. It's not for lack of trying, but I find myself at the boiling point and I can't keep my mouth shut. I feel the need to scream, and even if the scream is not answered, I find my sanity in the echo.

This all may seem very bleak. But I do have my friends, and they have been more than kind—generous to a fault. They have served me in good stead and have put up with me for reasons I cannot comprehend. They have provided me with shelter from the many storms I have mentioned; and as awful as it all may seem, they are the reason I believe that all will be well. But if not, we can at least laugh about it.

My friends are and have been my extended family through the years; and though the faces may have changed over time, they are all immutably a part of my DNA. Many Americans believe that there is only one type of family unit, and it is based entirely on blood and heterosexuality. Well, like it or not, the rules have changed. The people who cling to rhetoric about "family values" are the folks who can't live without hardbound rules. They worship them at times more than God. They take great joy in embracing their anachronisms as much as I do my anarchism. That anarchism isn't meant to be a threat to their lives, it's just the way that I have responded to the fates.

I have been blessed with great friends, and they are the indisputable good fortune of my life. They are the ones who have kept the door open to my sanity, for they are the ones who say, "Lewis, stop it now, that's crazy."

I have tried to give you the dots that somehow connected until I became who I have become. Keep your eyes open and don't be afraid of the darkness. You are not crazy. They are.

Who are "they"? It's tough to say. It may change from day to day, but there is a "they," and they are so powerful they really don't give a shit what we think anymore. But

I'm going to stop talking about them. Not that I'm paranoid or anything like that—it's just that maybe they published this book. Remember, when it comes to them, you can never be too safe.

The good news is . . . the road never ends. And it's not over till it's over. Happy trails.

ACKNOWLEDGMENTS

I would like to thank everyone on this list. They each deserve a chapter. So write your own book. (If I forgot anyone, and I no doubt have, my humblest apologies.) Ed Wasserman, Stanley Pomerantz, Louise Bloch, Ken Beard, Ryan Fried, the Simmons Family, the Kaplans, the Greenwalds, the Chaikens, the Sullivan Clan, The Clarkes, Miss Hoon, Mrs. Graves, Jeff Emerson, Ray Larson, Lenny Hughes, Cliff Figallo, Cynthia Coleman, Don Smith, Cary Engleberg, Tom Fiore, Rick Redcay, David Peace, Natalie Munson, Smitty, Sue and Judy Hunt, Dave Larson, Hazel and R.D. Larson, Pam Reed, Becky Davis, Charley Rock, Marcia Horner, Gary Wasserman, the Class of '66 of Springbrook High School, Jeff Davis, Charley Huntley, H.B. Hough, Whit and Sharon Andrews, Gayle Behrman, Leon Padula, Susan Berman, Mary Pope, Roger Howell, Malcolm Groome, Homer Foyle, Cindy Champion, Roy and Jane Underhill, Rick and Carla Gibbs, George Ceres, Mitch and Ginny Albright, the Guys at Pilam, John Coleman, Hal Fisher, Rick Young, Gail Craddock, Michael Tucker, Kai Jurgenson, Will Geer, Shyanne, Eric, Tom Schall, Jim Mathes, James and Marylin Yoshimura, Caitlin Clarke, Tommy Gardner, Peter Blanc, R.N. Sandberg, Ed Gold, Ted Talley, Richard Gilman, Jeremy Geidt, Bill Peters, Paul Schiehorn, Joe Grifasi, John McAndrew, David Marshall Grant, Peter Crombie, Becky Nelson, Jim Ingalls, Grace McKeaney, Mark Milliken, Warren and Nancy Glazer, Spike Whaley, Ben Halley Jr., the Class of '77 of the Yale School of Drama, Rand Foerster, Mark Linn Baker, Neil Mazzella, Drew McCoy, Tony Shaloub,

Tommy Derrah, Kristine Neilson, Bill Foeller, Michael Ritchie, Kate Burton, Sybil Burton Christopher, Steve Olsen, Dan Schlissel, Dale Davis, Jay Tarses, Don Scardino, Shannon Kennedy, Dee Sandt, Bill Hatch, Tommy Slaughter, Laura Grey, Dr. Martha Harrell, Elizabeth Keiser, Rowan Joseph, Dawn Steinberg, Gaylin Ross, Julie Hays, Jennifer Dallas, Steve Fisher and the folks at APA, John Moonvess, Matt Lichtenberg, Jon Stewart, the gang at *The Daily Show* and Comedy Central for all their support, Jules Feiffer, Dave Hart, Geoff Wills, Bruce McVittie, Carol Ochs, Willie Reale, Jenny Gersten, Kathleen Madigan, Dave Attell, Liz Winstead, Jeff Stilson, Dom Irrera, Dan Ballard, Judy Gold, Mike Wilmot, Will and Debbie Durst, Scott Blakeman, Jimmy Tingle, Susie Essman, Joy Behar, John Bowman and the hundreds of comics I have worked with, Frank Moreno, Benjamin Brewer, Bjorn Wentlandt, Alison Fraser and Rusty Magee, Robert Brustein, John McMartin, Kevin O'Rourke, Sam Diego, Tom Fontana, Bruce Paltrow, Roger Paul, Joe Cacaci, Shelly Berman, George Carlin, Lenny Bruce, Paul Krassner, Richard Belzer, Franz Kotterer, Joseph Heller, Kimber Rickabaugh and Paul Miller, Jack Rollins, The Friar's Club, Rick Newman and the original Catch A Rising Star in NYC, Caroline Hirsch and Caroline's Comedy Club, Chris Mazzilli and the Gotham Comedy Club, Lucien Hold and the Comic Strip, the Improvs in D.C., Baltimore, San Jose, Tampa Bay, Tempe, and Los Angeles, The Punchlines of San Francisco and Atlanta, the Acme Comedy Club, Joey and Stooges, the maniacs at El Brookmans in Anacostia, Cobbs Comedy Club in San Francisco, the Omaha Funny Bone, Zanies in Chicago, Vernon Hills, and

Nashville, Talmadge Reagan, Judy Chesnutt, The Comedy Connection in Boston, The Comedy Stop at the Trop in Vegas and Atlantic City, Stanford and Sons in Kansas City, The Irish, New Zealand, Montreal, Chicago, Boston and HBO Comedy Festivals, Bob Babisch and Punky and Milwaukee's Summerfest, the Magic Theatre, the Kenyon Festival Theatre, Ensemble Studio Theatre, the West Bank Cafe and Downstairs Theatre Bar and all the folks who ever worked there, the Williamstown Theatre Festival, the Fifty-Second Street Project, all of my friends at the Cystic Fibrosis Foundation, Mark and Joanne, Tricia, and Hank.